GW01374777

Psychic

A Psychic Development Guide for Tapping into Your Ability for Telepathy, Mediumship, Intuition, Aura Reading, Clairvoyance, Healing and Communicating with Your Spirit Guides

© **Copyright 2020**

All Rights Reserved. No part of this book may be reproduced in any form without permission in writing from the author. Reviewers may quote brief passages in reviews.

Disclaimer: No part of this publication may be reproduced or transmitted in any form or by any means, mechanical or electronic, including photocopying or recording, or by any information storage and retrieval system, or transmitted by email without permission in writing from the publisher.

While all attempts have been made to verify the information provided in this publication, neither the author nor the publisher assumes any responsibility for errors, omissions or contrary interpretations of the subject matter herein.

This book is for entertainment purposes only. The views expressed are those of the author alone, and should not be taken as expert instruction or commands. The reader is responsible for his or her own actions.

Adherence to all applicable laws and regulations, including international, federal, state and local laws governing professional licensing, business practices, advertising and all other aspects of doing business in the US, Canada, UK or any other jurisdiction is the sole responsibility of the purchaser or reader.

Neither the author nor the publisher assumes any responsibility or liability whatsoever on the behalf of the purchaser or reader of these materials. Any perceived slight of any individual or organization is purely unintentional.

Your Free Gift (only available for a limited time)

Thanks for getting this book! If you want to learn more about various spirituality topics, then join Mari Silva's community and get a free guided meditation MP3 for awakening your third eye. This guided meditation mp3 is designed to open and strengthen ones third eye so you can experience a higher state of consciousness. Simply visit the link below the image to get started.

https://spiritualityspot.com/meditation

Contents

INTRODUCTION 1

CHAPTER 1: THE PSYCHIC: WHAT DOES IT MEAN TO BE PSYCHIC? 3

CHAPTER 2: MEDITATION: THE FIRST STEP 12

CHAPTER 3: INTUITION 22

CHAPTER 4: THE CLAIRS: CLAIRVOYANCE, CLAIRAUDIENCE, CLAIRGUSTANCE, CLAIRCOGNIZANCE AND CLAIRSENTIENCE 32

CHAPTER 5: TELEPATHY 44

CHAPTER 6: MEDIUMSHIP 53

CHAPTER 7: PSYCHOMETRY 62

CHAPTER 8: AURA READING 69

CHAPTER 9: HEALING 79

CHAPTER 10: CONTACTING AND COMMUNICATING WITH YOUR SPIRIT GUIDES 86

CONCLUSION 96

SOURCES 98

Introduction

Fascination with psychic abilities is something that has been on the rise in recent years. An ever-growing number of people are exploring topics that were relatively unheard of or considered taboo not that long ago. Things such as clairvoyance, telepathy, intuition, and even communicating with spirits are becoming more mainstream, with an increasing number of scientific experiments and case studies supporting the conclusion that these phenomena are demonstrably real. Even so, it is the fact that countless people are awakening to their psychic abilities that underlie the growing interest in such topics. More and more people are discovering certain inherent talents, ones that enable them to do things beyond what conventional wisdom would suggest is possible. The problem is that most of these people don't know the true nature of their abilities, nor how to harness and strengthen them, resulting in those talents largely going to waste.

Fortunately, the process of discovering and developing psychic abilities is far easier than most people realize. The truth of the matter is that everyone has psychic abilities of one form or another; they simply need to identify which ones they possess in order to begin fulfilling their full potential. This book will reveal how to determine what psychic abilities you possess, thereby enabling you to discover your inherent skills. It will also explore the numerous forms that psychic ability takes, showing you the differences and similarities between each of them. Finally, this book will delve into the methods and techniques for developing whatever psychic ability you possess. Everything from meditation techniques to instructions on how to communicate with spirits is covered, providing you with every tool necessary to begin your journey into the exciting and fulfilling world of psychic phenomena. By the time you finish reading this book, you will know exactly what talents you possess and how to develop those talents in order to transform your life into the happy and fulfilling one you both desire and deserve.

Chapter 1: The Psychic: What Does It Mean to Be Psychic?

The term "psychic" is one that almost everyone has heard at one point or another. One of the first images that may come to mind is that of an exotic woman promising to tell you what the future holds for only ten dollars a minute—a real bargain considering what's at stake. Another image might be of a person using their psychic abilities to tell what card a member of the audience is holding or to levitate a table in front of that same audience. Needless to say, most of these examples of psychic abilities are nothing more than parlor tricks, more often than not found in the same books that teach a person how to pull a rabbit out of a hat. Unfortunately, this false and hokey image of what a psychic is causes most people to dismiss the real phenomenon, one that affects virtually every single person daily. This results in countless people failing ever to tap into their true psychic potential and use their abilities to transform their lives. Therefore, it is important to properly define what it means to be psychic, thereby helping you to discover your abilities and talents.

What does the Term "Psychic" Really Mean?

Perhaps the best way to understand what the term "psychic" really means is to take a closer look at the word itself. The word comes from the Greek word "psyche", which means mind or soul. This is also the root word for such things as psychology, psychiatry, and psychosomatic. All of these words share a common meaning, namely the focus on the mind as opposed to the physical body. Anyone with a psychological condition is understood to have a problem emotionally or mentally, and thus in need of treatment that focuses on the heart and mind. The very same thing holds true for someone with psychic abilities. In this case, rather than having a negative condition, such a person will have special skills relating to their emotional and mental perception of the world around them. In short, someone with psychic abilities can gain information or perform a task without using their five physical senses.

Numerous ancient traditions embrace the notion that the soul of a person has the same sensory capabilities as that of their body. In other words, just as the body can see and hear, so too, the soul of an individual can also see and hear, albeit without having to rely on physical hearing or sight. Not only does this enable a person to see beyond their physical space or hear beyond the range of physical hearing, but it also enables them to see things that would otherwise be invisible and hear things that would otherwise be silent. Thoughts, for example, cannot be heard with the physical ear since they make no physical sound. However, they can be heard with the "mind's ear" since they exist in the realm of the mind. The ability to hear things with the mind is known as clairaudience, which means "clear hearing".

The same phenomenon can be found in terms of seeing. Clairvoyance, or "clear seeing", is the ability to see with the mind. This allows a person to see beyond what their physical eyes can perceive. Such things as future events, far away events, or even the intentions of another person can be seen with the mind's eye. Another term that is used to describe such abilities is "supernatural", which in its purest definition means "above natural". Unfortunately, this term has also come to mean many different things, resulting in more confusion than clarification when used. However, in its truest form, supernatural simply implies that an event or ability is beyond what the five physical or natural senses can achieve. This is perhaps the best and most concise definition of psychic phenomena and abilities that can be found.

One of the most common mistakes many people make is to assume that all psychic abilities are essentially the same. A good example of this can be seen in the area of mediumship. A medium is someone who can convey messages and visions to a person by tapping into the spirit realm. More often than not, such individuals are labeled as fortune tellers, and thus dismissed as tricksters and fakes. Another term often used to categorize such individuals is that of psychic. Herein lies a very important distinction. While all mediums are psychics, not all psychics are mediums. It's a bit like saying that while all Californians are Americans, not all Americans are Californians. Not only do the vast majority of Americans not live in California, but most have never even visited the state. The very same thing holds true for psychics. A person can have psychic abilities but not be able to read a person's mind or see far off events. The fact of the matter is that there are numerous different categories of psychic abilities, each with even their own unique skills and qualities, making it so that almost no two psychics are exactly the same.

Who has Psychic Potential?

This distinction is vital when it comes to being able to determine your unique psychic abilities. Just because you don't have vivid dreams, or you can't sense what another person is thinking is no reason to believe that you have no abilities whatsoever. Again, there are numerous different types of psychic abilities, and thus it is important to keep an open mind when trying to discover your personal potential. The bottom line is that everyone has psychic potential of one form or another. This is because everyone is, in essence, a spirit being, or a soul. Therefore, just as anyone with a physical body will have physical senses, so too, anyone with a spirit or a soul will have psychic abilities. The trick is to discover what abilities you possess in abundance.

Once again, this is another example of how psychic senses and physical senses are a direct reflection of one another. Although everyone has a physical body, that doesn't mean that everyone has the same eyesight or the same ability to hear sound. While some people have very keen eyesight, allowing them to read extra fine print or to see something far away with great clarity and detail, others require reading glasses to see that fine print, or prescription glasses to see far off distances. Others still may not be able to see at all, forcing them to rely on their other physical senses in order to perceive the world around them. A blind person may use their sense of touch to help them read, as in the case of Braille, or to visualize what a person looks like. This is precisely how psychic abilities work as well. Just because everyone has a soul, it doesn't mean that everyone can read minds or predict the future. While some may possess such skills in high degrees, others will find themselves virtually blind and deaf in such areas.

Needless to say, the important thing isn't necessarily to fix the wrong things. Rather than trying to develop skill sets that you lack or that you struggle with, the trick is to discover your strengths and develop them to the highest level possible. A good way to envision this is to imagine a baseball team. A good coach allows the pitcher to hone their pitching skills while allowing their best hitters to hone their batting skills. You wouldn't see a pitcher being made to improve their batting, nor a hitter forced to develop pitching skills. The name of the game is to play everyone to their strengths. That holds true for psychic abilities. If you can't see auras, then don't waste your time trying to develop the skill. Instead, find the skill you currently have, the one that is inherent to your abilities. Once you find that, the next step is to nurture it and develop it so that it can serve you in your day-to-day life, thereby taking your life to a whole new level.

That said, some people are indeed more gifted than others when it comes to psychic abilities. Fortunately, there are a few simple tests that can help to identify whether a person is gifted with strong psychic abilities or not. One such test is in the area of dreams. If you have a rich dream life, wherein you experience vivid and engaging dreams regularly, the chances are that you have strong psychic abilities. In fact, the ability to recall dreams is another indicator of psychic potential. If you often have gut feelings, such as to avoid certain people or situations, then you are probably a natural psychic. Visions of future events, the ability to feel another person's emotions, or read their thoughts are also signs of heightened psychic ability. The reason that such events indicate psychic potential is that they all rely on no physical senses. Thus, a person who can dream vividly and recall their dreams uses their mind's eye in a very real way. Someone who has gut feelings is in touch with their intuition, and so on. You are probably reading this book because you have discovered a pattern in your life, one in which your psychic ability has shown itself and is now waiting for you to respond and give it the attention it deserves.

How can Psychic Abilities Impact your Day-to-Day Life?

Like any abilities, psychic abilities can be used in a vast number of ways to improve and even transform a person's day-to-day life. One example of this is in the area of intuition. Many people have to make decisions daily that will impact their lives in one way or another. They might have to buy a car, look for a job, or even hire a person to work for them. Although a good deal of factual information is usually available to help in making such decisions, there can also be a fair amount of guesswork involved. This is where intuition can make all the difference. Rather than having to guess whether or not you will be happy in a given job, or whether a candidate is truly as good as their résumé makes them appear to be, you can use intuition to see beyond the facts and determine the truth of a situation. This can help you to make the best choice every time, avoiding mistakes and regrets that can undermine your happiness or even your very chance of success.

Dreams can also come in handy when making all-important decisions. Many people have heard someone say, "Let me sleep on it," at one time or another. Although this statement usually indicates a person's desire to give a decision some extra thought, the truth is that someone with psychic abilities could literally "sleep on it", allowing their dreams to reveal the outcome of one decision or another. Such practices have been recorded throughout human history in virtually every corner of the globe. Using dreams to make decisions or understand the nature of complex events can help you to cheat by literally skipping ahead to see what awaits down each path at your disposal. This can not only take away the guesswork to a decision, but it can also ensure that you make the best decision every single time. Furthermore, numerous case studies have revealed how inventors, artists, and musicians have used their dreams to solve problems or unlock their true potential. Not only *can* such an ability be the difference between success and failure, but it has been proven.

Intuition can also help you to engage more meaningfully with those around you, thereby improving your relationships in a very real and significant way. A good example of this is in the area of empathy. An empath is someone who can tap into the emotions of another person, virtually feeling what they feel. One way this can help is to protect you from those who would cheat or deceive you, such as corrupt business people, false friends, or anyone who would seek to take advantage of you. By feeling another person's emotional state, you can determine their sincerity or lack thereof. However, the main application for empathy is the ability to know how a person feels so that you can better connect with them and help them through their time of struggle. By sharing another person's pain, you can prove more capable when it comes to saying the right thing or even giving the best advice. This ability will help you to feel connected to everyone around you in a way that will transform how you experience life itself. No longer will you feel as though you are an individual, making your way alone through life. Instead, you will understand that all living beings are connected, and this will make you realize that no one is ever truly alone.

Establishing Rules to Ensure Better Control of your Abilities

Of course, it goes without saying that strong abilities bring strong responsibilities. Nowhere is this notion truer than in the area of psychic abilities. Subsequently, it is absolutely vital that in addition to discovering and honing your abilities, you also establish a set of rules that will serve to protect you as well as those around you. Without such rules, you will inevitably find yourself in a situation in which others can cause you harm or in which you bring harm to others. Since psychic abilities come from the soul, such harm would be felt on the soul level, making it that much harder to recover from. Therefore, preventing such incidents is critical as it will enable you to avoid considerable hardship and regret all around.

One of the most important rules is that of giving yourself the time and space you need to recharge your batteries. More often than not, people who discover and develop their psychic abilities do so intending to help others around them. The ability to connect to the feelings of others, heal the pains and ills of others, or even tap into the spirit realm to foretell another person's destiny are all noble pursuits, but they all come at a cost. Every psychic activity takes energy to perform, much like every purchase you make requires cash. As such, if you aren't careful, you can use up all of your energy trying to save the world, just like you can spend all of your money if you go on a shopping spree. Therefore, the trick is to budget yourself when it comes to the time and energy you spend helping others. One of the best rules is to give yourself plenty of downtime daily or fairly regularly, thereby enabling you to recharge your batteries and restore tranquility to your mind. This will keep you from becoming burned out, or even worse, depressed and overwhelmed.

Another critical rule to employ is that of respecting other people's privacy. Just because you can read another person's thoughts doesn't mean you should. Nor does it mean that they want you to. A good rule of thumb that will help you to respect others is only to use your abilities when it is necessary for your personal wellbeing. Thus, tapping into the heart or mind of someone trying to sell you a car or applying for a job is perfectly reasonable. Reading the mind of the person sitting next to you on the bus for kicks, on the other hand, is less than decent. Therefore, only ever use your abilities in a way that is necessary and beneficial to all involved. Never abuse your skills, and never use them to intimidate others.

Some Examples of Real Psychic Events

While almost everyone contemplates psychic abilities at one time or another, most dismiss their existence altogether, citing a lack of evidence to support their existence. Fortunately, there are a growing number of case studies and personal accounts that will offer the evidence needed to inspire people to take psychic phenomena more seriously. The following are just a few examples of real-life psychic events, some that changed lives on a personal level, while others changed the world as we know it.

One story involves a journalist who was interviewing a medium for a story. After the interview, the medium offered a free reading for the journalist. Although skeptical, she agreed, not knowing what to expect. Immediately the medium told her of a woman that he saw, one whose description and name matched that of her long-dead grandmother. Next, he told her of a man with the woman, and the description matched that of her more recently departed father. The man had a message for his wife, the medium said. That message was that it was time to get rid of his neckties. After the reading, the journalist called her mother and asked if she had gotten rid of her father's clothes yet, something she had hesitated to do. The mother said she had gotten rid of everything *except* his neckties.

Another story involves a man who had gone AWOL from the army while serving in Vietnam. While on shore leave back in the States, he decided to not return to duty. During that time, he visited a friend who was skilled at divination. He conducted an I Ching reading, which revealed that a long trip over a great body of water would prove beneficial. The friend decided to go back to Vietnam, despite wanting to leave the army. Upon his return, the number of troops in Vietnam was reduced, and he was given a regular discharge, allowing him to leave the army and return home legally.

Dreams have served to shape decisions and discoveries, many of which have changed the world in ways most people don't realize. Elias Howe, for example, struggled with designing the mechanical sewing machine. After several failed attempts, he was almost bankrupt when one night, he dreamt of where the needle needed to go in order for the machine to work properly. Upon waking, he drew the design, a design that became patented and is still used in modern sewing machine models today.

Niels Bohr, a pioneer in modern physics, had a dream in which he saw the planets orbiting the sun. He realized that this dream was the answer to his search for the model of an atom. Using his dream imagery, he was able to prove the structure of the atom, which is responsible for shaping such things as atomic energy. Albert Einstein dreamt of an experience in which he was sledding downhill on a snowy mountain. He began going so fast that he almost reached the speed of light. At that moment, the appearance of the stars changed, leading him to discover the Theory of Relativity.

Countless more examples of dreams, readings, visions, and the like that have changed lives can be found all around the world. However, such stories are in the end just that—stories. The important thing is to find your own proof, your own evidence. Fortunately, everyone has had experiences that they can't explain in simple, natural terms. Those experiences are the fingerprints of psychic activity, usually involving their personal psychic abilities. Rather than looking to other accounts as proof, you should look to them for direction, helping you to recall and recognize the evidence you have within your life, the evidence of your psychic potential.

Chapter 2: Meditation: The First Step

One of the principal tools for developing psychic abilities is the practice of meditation. This practice has been around for thousands of years, helping countless people around the world to achieve numerous benefits and breakthroughs. In fact, tradition states that the Buddha himself achieved enlightenment as a result of his meditative practices. Fortunately, you don't need to be searching for truth or enlightenment to make use of this valuable tool. Millions of people around the world today use enlightenment for various reasons, including everything from spiritual development to stress relief and physical restoration. This chapter will provide a basic understanding of what meditation is, as well as the various ways in which it can help you to nurture and hone your psychic skills. Furthermore, there will be instructions on a few forms of meditation to help you get started with a practice that will provide you with a solid foundation for your quest to become a proficient psychic.

A Basic Overview of Meditation

When most people think of meditation, they envision Buddhist monks dressed in their robes, chanting as they allow their minds to transcend physical reality and touch the realm of spirit. While this is one aspect of meditation, it is not the be-all and end-all of the practice. A good way to understand meditation is to think of it as a gym of sorts. When you go to a gym, you can choose to do any number of exercise routines, ranging from free weights, aerobic exercises, general strength training, or even just getting on an exercise bike or a treadmill to shake up an otherwise sedentary life. Each type of routine offers specific benefits and results, meaning that no two people will necessarily have the same experience. This is precisely how meditation works.

Overall, the fundamentals of meditation are generally the same from one form to another, despite the numerous and distinct differences that make each form very unique. The basic premise is that the practitioner finds a quiet location where they can be alone and uninterrupted for a specified period. Within that period, they will begin to shut out external influences and distractions, focusing on their internal reality instead. More often than not, breathing plays a central role in the practice, providing the individual with a focus point that enables them to achieve the calm and mindful state they are aiming for. Sitting in a comfortable yet upright position is also central to just about all forms of meditation. Beyond that, however, the other elements tend to be specific to the various versions, thereby creating a different experience that allows a person to achieve different results.

Mindfulness, for example, is a common goal shared by most practitioners of meditation. Certain forms of meditation allow you to develop your sense of mental focus and clarity, removing the clutter that fills most people's minds daily. Relaxation is another benefit that comes from most forms of meditation, including that known as body scan meditation. This form is also used to send healing and restorative energy to parts of the body that are suffering in one way or another. In short, there are two main categories of meditation: calming and insightful. Calming meditation is those techniques that focus on stress relief of both the body and mind. Alternatively, insightful meditation techniques are those that focus on sharpening mental and physical awareness.

There is one more distinction worth mentioning in terms of the different forms of meditative practice, namely that of guided and unguided meditation. Guided meditation simply suggests that you practice under the instruction of a guide. That guide can be an actual person, such as a spiritual instructor, or it can be a pre-recorded message that takes you through the steps and helps you to understand the process every step of the way. Unguided meditation simply indicates that you perform your practice alone and in silence—at least in the case of those techniques that are practiced in solitude. It is often recommended that beginners engage in guided meditation first in order to better understand the practice. This also gives them the chance to ask questions or raise concerns in the event they meditate in the presence of an actual guide.

How Meditation Helps Develop Psychic Abilities

The question many people ask is how meditation can help develop psychic abilities. Truth be told, there are several ways in which meditative practices can help anyone to discover, nurture, and hone their psychic skills. One of the most immediate ways that meditation achieves this goal is that it helps the individual to clear their heart and mind of all the clutter and chaos that ordinarily affects them. This condition is commonly referred to as "monkey mind" in the Buddhist tradition. Simply put, most people have any number of thoughts, concerns, images, and even songs running through their minds at any given time. This noise only serves to make it harder to connect with intuition, insight, and other psychic abilities that require a mind that is calm and focused in order to be heard. By removing the noise, meditation can create the environment necessary for effective psychic activity.

Another way in which meditation helps to improve psychic abilities is to increase mental clarity and awareness. Techniques for achieving this goal fall under the insightful category. A person who practices insightful meditation will exercise their mind and awareness in a way that hones their ability to resist distractions and become aware of the energies within and around them. As mentioned earlier, all psychic activity involves the mind in one way or another. Therefore, any exercise that strengthens the mind and improves such things as focus, perception, and mental discipline will naturally strengthen a person's psychic abilities. In a way, it's a bit like when sports players go to the gym to work out. To the average person, it might seem strange that lifting weights could help someone play soccer better. However, to the athlete, it makes perfect sense since the stronger their body is, the better their performance on the pitch. Meditation is exactly like that. It strengthens the muscles needed to perform psychic activities to the best of a person's abilities.

The third and least known way that meditation helps to develop psychic abilities is that it helps a person connect with their inner voice. Whether the goal is to shut out external distractions or to eliminate internal noise, the outcome of meditation is largely the same, namely an increased sense of intuition. After all, once all the distraction is gone, the only thing left is the true voice of the individual. This voice is that which is referred to as intuition, or a person's gut feeling. The stronger this voice becomes, the stronger a person's psychic abilities become. Additionally, meditation can help an individual to connect to their spirit guides. Just as hearing the inner voice is essential for psychic practice, so too, hearing the voice of spirit guides is equally critical. Therefore, meditation is a crucial tool as it helps a person to discover and connect to that part of them that is the very heart of any psychic ability. Added to the increase of mindfulness and the decrease of distraction, it's no wonder that the most effective psychics are those who practice meditation regularly, if not daily.

How to Perform Mindfulness Meditation

Mindfulness meditation allows a person to develop their ability to be fully present in the moment. This is vital for anyone who wants to tap into their intuition for guidance or answers. Furthermore, it is a good way to help a person tune in to their spirit guides. The steps for performing mindfulness meditation are as follows:

- The first step for just about every meditation practice is to find a quiet place where you can be alone and uninterrupted for a specified period. This will help you to focus on your practice as you won't be distracted or even listening for potential distractions to occur.

• When you have your location picked out, the next thing you need to do is to sit comfortably. Sitting cross-legged on a cushion or mat on the floor is ideal, but not necessary. A chair will also suffice provided it allows you to sit upright, keeping a good posture that allows for good, deep breathing. The important thing is to keep your spine straight, thus allowing your breath and energy to flow evenly throughout your body. Your upper arms should hang loosely by your side while your hands can be allowed to rest in your lap in whatever way feels most comfortable.

• Next, you need to start focusing on your breathing. Begin to take deeper breaths, ones that are relaxing and restorative. Although your goal is to breathe deeper, your breathing should still be natural and unforced, thereby increasing relaxation to your body and mind.

• Once your breathing is regulated, the next step is to become aware of your surroundings. Take a moment to recognize the sights, sounds, and even smells of your environment. However, don't allow your thoughts to dwell on one thing for too long. The goal is to become aware, nothing more, nothing less. Therefore, observe one thing or event for about ten seconds, then move on to another.

• Your mind will begin to fixate on things from time to time, evoking memories or judgments depending on the item or event you are observing. Whenever this happens, simply let go of the thought process and return to simply observing your surroundings. The most important thing is to be wholly present in body and mind.

• Finally, recognize that your mind is simply doing its job by dredging up thoughts, concerns, and memories based on what you are observing. This isn't a bad thing as such, merely a habit that you are beginning to break. Don't be too harsh on yourself whenever this happens. Simply allow your distracting thoughts to evaporate and return your focus to your present moment. The more you practice this form of meditation, the less distracted your mind will become.

- Once you have perfected the skill of directing your mind from distraction to the here and now you can begin to practice mindfulness meditation in a more public setting. The same principles apply, except now you can shift your attention from one person to another or from one event to another, allowing yourself to observe without judging or becoming fixated on any one thing or person. Needless to say, never perform this kind of exercise while driving a car or operating machinery that requires your full attention.

How to Perform Visualization Meditation

Visualization meditation is a practice that helps an individual hone their ability to connect to objects and people remotely. This means you can see a person or a thing without having to be anywhere near them. Needless to say, such a vision involves the mind's eye rather than the physical eye. The steps for performing visualization meditation are as follows:

- Find a quiet place where you will be alone and uninterrupted for the time you need for your meditative practice. It is important to establish how long you want to spend so that you ensure yourself the best chance for success.
- Sit in a cross-legged position with your spine straight, your upper arms relaxed by your sides, and your hands resting comfortably in your lap. This posture will help to relax your body and improve your breathing and blood flow, thus increasing your mental awareness.
- Once you have achieved a comfortable position, you can begin to establish your deep, relaxed breathing routine. Start taking longer, deeper breaths, ones that relax you while

providing the oxygen needed to restore your physical and mental energies.

• The next step is for beginners. This step has you observe an object in front of you. It can be any object at all, and you can pick and choose an object to meditate on to make it easier. Simply stare at the object for a minute or so, taking in every detail you can.

• Next, close your eyes and begin to visualize the object you observed. Allow your mind to recall all of the details you can remember, using your imagination to recreate the object in as much detail as possible. You can even imagine yourself moving around the object, seeing it from all sides. However, you should remain seated, only moving in your mind.

• Once you have clearly visualized your chosen object, you can begin to visualize something else. This can be another object, such as something else in the room, or even something elsewhere, such as your car or your neighbor's mailbox. Alternatively, you can choose to visualize a person, picturing them where you imagine them to be. No matter what you choose to visualize, the trick is to visualize your subject with as much detail as possible, even allowing yourself to observe the surroundings.

• Next, start to take note of the specific details you notice. For example, if you visualize your neighbor's mailbox, is the flag up or down? Is the sky clear or cloudy? What specific features can you pick out? In the case of a person, where are they? Are they at home or work? Are they talking to a person, working on the computer, or making a phone call? How do they appear emotionally? All of these details can prove important in terms of psychic ability. While your mind might begin by using memory to create the vision of a person or object, eventually, it will connect to the subject in real-time, allowing you to observe things in your mind's eye that your physical senses would be unable to detect.

- Finally, take note of any specific details that stand out. If you envision a person and you see them having a bad day, call them later and ask them how their day was. Again, initial results may be irregular, but over time, you will discover that your observations will become more and more accurate, enabling you to connect to any object or person without having to leave the comfort of your home.

How to Perform Psychic Meditation

Psychic meditation is the form of meditation that really allows a person to tap into their psychic skills. Specifically, it hones a person's ability to see, feel, and hear information on the spirit level. Images, whispers, sensations, and the like all become more regular and more pronounced the more a person practices psychic meditation. The steps for performing psychic meditation are as follows:

- As with any form of meditation, the first step is always to find a quiet place that offers privacy as well as solitude. Unplug any phones and remove any other forms of distraction, ensuring the most peaceful environment possible.
- Next, sit on the floor, using a mat or a cushion for comfort, in a cross-legged position. Although you want to be relaxed, it is vital to ensure that your spine is straight, as this will increase blood and oxygen flow throughout the body. Again, your upper arms should hang freely by your sides, and your hands should be relaxed in your lap.
- Once you have your location and posture sorted, the next step is to focus on your breathing, ensuring your breaths are deep but relaxed, not forced or strained. As you focus on your breathing, allow your body to relax and clear your mind of any extra thoughts or distractions.
- Next, close your eyes and begin to observe any images, feelings, sounds, or impulses that occur out of the blue. At first, you might find your mind still full of thoughts and

images from your day's activities. If this is the case, take more time to focus on your breathing and thus clear your mind of clutter and noise. However, once your mind is clear, any images, sounds, and the like should be observed and contemplated.

- Take the time to consider every impulse you get, whether it's a physical sensation, an emotional reaction, or an image, word, or some other form of information, no matter how random it may seem. In fact, the more random it is, the more likely it is to be psychic in nature rather than the product of your imagination. If you feel an emotion, take the time to consider what the emotion is and what might be causing it. Is it a warning? Is it for someone else? Or is someone thinking about you? If you see an image of a friend or a loved one, contemplate that image carefully. Are they happy, or are they in need of your love and support? The important thing is to open your mind to all input from the spirit realm. Again, at first, you might struggle to differentiate between figments of your imagination and the voice of your spirit guides. However, with practice, the ability to know the difference will strengthen, allowing you to hear the voice of the Universe as clearly as you hear a voice on the other end of a phone.
- Once you have ended your meditation, you must take the time to reconnect to your immediate surroundings. This will close your mind to the constant flow of information that would otherwise overwhelm you as you go about your regular day. The best way to achieve this goal is to practice a short round of mindfulness meditation, thereby reconnecting to your environment and restoring your mind to its normal function.
- The two most important things to remember concerning psychic meditation are to be open-minded and patient. Only by being open-minded can you receive the information you are seeking. And only by being patient can you develop your

skills to the level you desire. Nothing worth doing is ever easy, so don't be frustrated if results are slow and erratic. With a little effort and patience, you will begin to achieve the results you desire, and then your psychic abilities will rise to levels you never imagined possible.

Improving Meditation with Yoga

One way to take your meditation practice to the next level is to incorporate it with the practice of yoga. This helps align your body and mind in a way that creates a certain singularity of being. The more singular you are as a person is the clearer and more present you are at any given time. Therefore, it is recommended that once you have gained familiarity and even success with meditation, you should begin to add yoga to your routine to increase your abilities even further.

The basic principle of yoga is to stretch the body to improve blood flow and oxygen flow to all parts of the body, including the brain. This will have profound effects on your physical health and wellbeing as well as your mental health and wellbeing. Fortunately, there are many different forms of yoga, each designed for specific needs. Some are relatively easy, making it ideal for beginners or anyone with physical restrictions. Additionally, low-level yoga can be practiced alone, at home, and in very short amounts of time. Intermediate and high-level yoga should initially be practiced under the supervision of a certified instructor. You can start practicing alone once you are more experienced. Countless online resources will help you to get started with practicing yoga, thus enabling you to get a feel for it in order to see what forms are right for you. Additionally, the widespread practice of yoga means that there are groups virtually everywhere, allowing you to get the supervision you need as a beginner or as someone who likes to share their experience with others.

Chapter 3: Intuition

If you ask the average person on the street whether or not they have ever had a "gut feeling" about a person, place, or situation that proved to be true, almost everyone will tell you they have. This phenomenon is so common that few people ever pay any attention to it. Unfortunately, this means that only a handful of individuals take the time to discover the true nature of that gut feeling, including where it comes from, how it could be so accurate, and how to hone it for future use. In the end, this enigmatic gut feeling is but one example of intuition.

The simple fact of the matter is that intuition is the very language of the soul. It is how the soul communicates to the conscious and intellectual mind of an individual. As mentioned earlier, every person has both physical and non-physical senses, all of which send information to a person regarding their life, environment, and the choices at hand. Just as thoughts transmit physical information to the mind, intuition transmits non-physical information to the mind, providing insights far beyond what the physical senses can perceive. Understanding this language is the very foundation for developing any psychic ability. This chapter will explore the phenomenon of intuition, including its nature, the various forms it takes, methods for discovering and strengthening intuition, and some real-life examples of intuition at work. By the time you finish reading this chapter, you will have all the tools you need to begin tapping into your intuition, thereby discovering your full psychic potential.

What Exactly is Intuition?

Depending on whom you ask, intuition can mean any number of things. Some see it as a source of inherent knowledge, the ability to know something without having any logical or rational information to base that knowledge on. Others will define intuition as an inspiration of sorts, allowing a person to recognize opportunities as they arise or find solutions to problems that the intellect simply cannot provide. In the end, although these answers may seem vastly different, they are all correct. Intuition is the language that the soul uses to convey information to the mind. Therefore, whether the soul is telling the individual of upcoming opportunities, danger lurking around the corner, or some other necessary piece of information, intuition is the language it will use to convey the message.

Because intuition has many different faces, it has come to be called by many different names over time. In today's world, one of the most common names given to intuition is "gut feeling" or "gut instinct". Although the term "instinct" can mean something quite different from intuition, the way it is used to describe a feeling that acts as a warning, identifies it with intuition in this case. However, intuition has been known by other names throughout history and in the countless cultures that have spanned the globe. In Ancient Greece, a person's intuition was often seen as the voice of the gods themselves, offering divine inspiration or advice. Artists would attribute their intuitive abilities to the muses, while seers would give the Fates credit for the visions they had. It can be argued that the "voice of God" is another name for intuition, something that permeates Christian traditions all around the world today. In the end, no matter what culture or time you observe, you will find a widely recognized and respected phenomenon that clearly reflects intuition.

The real question is, "How does intuition affect psychic abilities?" To best understand this, you need to appreciate the value of language. If you were to move to another country, one that didn't speak English, the only way you would be able to get around in that country effectively would be to learn the language the natives spoke.

Until you learn their language, everything they say to you will sound like gibberish, while everything you say to them will seem equally strange to their ears. This is where learning a language can make all the difference. Once you study their words, you can begin to understand what they say, while also developing the ability to speak directly to them. Anyone who has ever lived abroad will know just how big the difference can be once you can communicate in the native tongue.

This same relationship exists between the conscious mind and the soul. No matter how hard a person tries, they will never be able to teach their soul to speak in logical, rational terms. Therefore, to communicate clearly with the soul, to understand what the soul has to say, it is vital to learn the language of intuition. Only then can you take the otherwise gibberish sounds, images, and feelings and translate them into the meaningful messages that they are. When you master the language of intuition, you can communicate with your soul and spirit guides in real-time, allowing you to receive and transmit valuable information across time and space, giving you untold advantages when it comes to living your day-to-day life. Fortunately, learning the language of intuition is far easier than learning an actual language with grammar, syntax, and many words and phrases to memorize. However, make no mistake; the language of intuition can prove to be the richest, most complex language you will ever come upon.

Who has Intuition?

If the biggest question about intuition is what its nature truly is, the second biggest question must necessarily be, "Who has intuition?" The answer is both simple and complex. In short, everyone has intuition. Every single living being has the language of the soul, since, in theory, every single living being has a soul. This means that every person has intuition at their disposal, whether they realize it or not. Furthermore, numerous studies have indicated that animals and even plants have measurable levels of intuition. Needless to say, this is a huge concept to wrap your mind around. However, if you recognize that the soul is the essence of life, then all living things must have a soul of sorts, and thus intuition to some degree.

What makes the answer to the question "Who has intuition?" complex is that intuition is not a static quantity. In other words, it's not like asking, "Who has a head?" or "Who can breathe air?" Both of those answers are fixed. Everyone has a head, and everyone can breathe, and for the most part, both of those things are largely equal from one person to the next. However, when it comes to intuition, the value is fluid in nature. A good way to understand this is to consider the question, "Who has muscles?" Well, everyone has muscles since muscles are an integral part of the human body. However, it is not true that everyone's muscles are equal or that everyone has the same potential for muscle development. The wimpy 100-pound kid walking past the gym does not have the same muscular build of the 250-pound bodybuilder in the gym. They both have the same muscles, but to different degrees and with different levels of potential. Even if the wimpy kid went into the gym and worked out, he may never reach the same levels as a bodybuilder with natural ability. This is precisely how intuition works.

In short, everyone is born with intuition, just like everyone is born with muscles. Some have a certain natural potential, giving them stronger intuition without even having to try, whereas others may have to struggle, or at the very least, work harder in order to develop their intuitive capabilities. Furthermore, those who put in the time and effort daily to develop and strengthen their intuition will become far stronger over time than those who don't. Therefore, while everyone has intuition, it doesn't mean that everyone can simply tell you what card you are holding, or tap into your long-departed relative's mind to convey a message they want you to hear. Such gifts are unique to specific individuals, and even then, they must be honed and nurtured to achieve their fullest effect. The trick is to discover your inherent potential concerning intuition, and then take the time to develop that potential to its fullest.

Different Forms of Intuition

As already discussed, not all intuitions are alike. Subsequently, there are many different "languages" spoken by the soul, each unique to the individual. Some people will be gifted with the ability to see things with their mind's eye, whereas others will be more gifted when it comes to "feeling their way" through a situation, making the right decisions without any forehand knowledge or experience. Fortunately, these various forms of intuition can be sorted into a few categories, making it easier to understand and manage. Although there are as many as six or seven different categories, depending on the tradition you explore, this section will deal with the four most common. These four forms are known as clairvoyance, clairaudience, clairsentience, and claircognizance.

Clairvoyance is the ability to see clearly with the mind's eye. Some people may consider this to be a form of imagination, and in truth, a person's imagination can have a great impact on their clairvoyant capabilities. However, the basic element of clairvoyance is the ability to see within the mind a person, place, or event as clearly as if you were observing those things with your physical eye. People with this ability can see future events, far off events, or even the faces of people whom they will see unexpectedly in the day to come. Simply put, clairvoyance is the visual language of the soul. It is when the soul sends a picture to the individual in an attempt to inform them of something significant. Most people dismiss such images as clutter in their minds, only to recall them later on, after the event or person in the image has presented themselves in real life. In contrast, those who recognize and develop this skill can use those images to be better prepared for the events about to unfold in their life, thus enabling them to take full advantage of those events when they happen.

Clairaudience is the language of intuition based on sound. Often referred to as a person's "inner voice", this is when the soul sends information to the person's mind in the form of spoken words. Needless to say, this isn't the same phenomenon as experienced by people having schizophrenic episodes where voices in their heads are telling them to commit atrocities; however, the voice of the soul can sound just as real to a person as the voice of their conscious mind. In fact, when a person develops their clairaudience to high levels, they can virtually have an internal dialogue between their conscious and subconscious mind, discussing and debating the issue at hand. The inner voice is perhaps the second most common form of intuition experienced by countless people all around the world. While some recognize it as intuition, others attribute it to God, guardian angels, spirit guides, and the like. The truth is that all of these things may be correct. Clairaudience simply indicates that a person receives intuitive thought through the spoken word. Where those words are spoken from is another conversation altogether.

If clairaudience is the second most popular form of intuition, *clairsentience* is probably the most common. This is when intuition takes the shape of a feeling, specifically a gut feeling. The term "I have a bad feeling about this" is all but cliché—having been used so many times and in many different settings. Even so, the reason it has been used so often comes down to that just about everyone can relate to it. Therefore, almost everyone has had an experience of clairsentience in their lifetime. More often than not, it comes when an individual has a good or bad feeling about someone else, giving them a direction when it comes to making decisions regarding that other person. In the case of having a bad feeling about someone, an individual can take better precautions in order to safeguard their wellbeing. Alternatively, in the event a person gets a good feeling about someone, it may indicate the potential for a thriving friendship, or in many cases, even marriage. What makes clairsentience significant is its almost perfect accuracy, demonstrating the very real nature of intuition and the information it has to offer.

Finally, there is *claircognizance*. This is perhaps the rarest of all forms of intuition, taking the shape of a person having an inherent knowledge of something they have no experience or training in. To the casual observer, it can appear as though a situation or an object simply reveals itself to a person with claircognizance, as if they were seeing an instruction manual no one else could see. Such a person may walk to where they need to be in a strange place without needing directions or a map. Alternatively, they may pick up a complex instrument and simply know how to use it, as though they had been using it their whole life. Individuals with this form of intuition are usually quick learners as they combine their cognitive skills with their intuition, allowing them to learn something both consciously and subconsciously at the same time. If you have ever just "known" a thing, an answer to a question, or how to perform a new task, you have probably tapped into your claircognizant potential without realizing it.

Some Examples of Real-Life Intuition

There are many examples of real-life intuition stories in which a person used their inherent knowledge to make a decision that later turned out to be highly important, even to the point of saving people's lives. One such example occurred when an airplane was sitting on the runway waiting to take off. A passenger heard a strange noise and became highly alarmed. At first, she addressed it with the other passengers around her, all of whom dismissed her concerns as nonsense. She eventually got the attention of the crew, who also assured her there was no need for concern. Undeterred, she refused to settle down until the plane was inspected. Upon inspection, a serious defect was discovered, one that would almost certainly have resulted in the plane crashing while in flight, potentially killing all on board. This example could fall under several categories of intuition, including clairaudience for hearing the sound, and clairsentience for having a bad feeling that simply would not go away.

Certain cultures treat intuition with far greater respect and acceptance, resulting in a seamless integration of intuition into day-to-day life. Perhaps the best example of this is Ayurvedic Medicine. This is the traditional form of medicine that has been practiced in

India for nearly five thousand years. It involves the doctor taking the patient's pulse using three fingers, enabling them to determine energy imbalances within the individual, as well as potential ways of treating them. This clearly mixes intellect with intuition, providing a more holistic approach to both illness and the methods for treating it. Needless to say, doctors in this tradition need to be as highly skilled in the psychic arts as they are in the science of medicine.

Unfortunately, most people have experienced intuition in the sense that they ignore the message they hear, only to discover its significance when it's too late. One example of this is when a woman needed to reach something on a high shelf in her home. As she grabbed a nearby chair to stand on, she heard a voice telling her not to use that chair, virtually shouting the warning to her. Dismissing the warning, she proceeded to stand on the chair, which immediately shattered under her, leaving her on the floor in pain with a dislocated elbow. While in the hospital, she vowed to always listen to that voice in the future as it had proven its value beyond any reasonable doubt.

How to Develop your Intuitive Abilities

Again, although everyone has intuitive abilities, those abilities need to be developed to be of any real value. This is no different than studying to learn a language, or putting in the time and effort to develop stronger muscles. Fortunately, the techniques for developing your intuitive abilities are fairly straightforward, requiring more time than actual effort to achieve your desired results. The following examples are a few of the more common and effective methods for strengthening your intuitive muscles.

One of the first things a person needs to do to develop intuitive abilities is to get in touch with their body. All too often, the noise and chaos filling the mind prevent an individual from hearing the message their body is sending them. Sometimes that message can come in the form of the proverbial gut feeling, but at other times, it can come in the form of sweaty palms, an increased heart rate, jitters, or any number of other physical symptoms that can serve as a warning of impending doom. To hear the message your intuition is sending, you must take the time to check how you feel physically throughout the day. This is particularly true if you are making a decision, whereby a negative physical reaction could serve as a warning to avoid a particular choice. It can also occur out of the blue, where your body just reacts to something yet to be experienced. The key is to take note of all the times your body reacts unusually. As you become more in tune with your body, you can begin to recognize the signals it is sending you, thereby using the information to avoid trouble or mistakes that can prove costly. Keeping a journal is one of the most effective ways of developing this connection. Write down any unusual feelings you get on a particular day, noting any experiences that correspond with those feelings. Eventually, you will discover the pattern between warning and reality, thus enabling you to recognize and use those warnings more effectively.

The same thing can be said concerning your inner voice. If you are the type of person who hears random statements, especially warnings or instructions, then you probably have a strong sense of clairaudience. To develop this strength, you need to start paying close attention to the messages you hear. Keeping a journal is an excellent way of developing this connection. As you write down the words you hear during a given day, you can also write down any events that occurred that might validate the message contained in those words. This will prove especially true in the event you ignore the words and suffer the consequences. As you record warnings that you ignored, along with the undesirable outcome, you will establish both a pattern and a sense of validation that will help you to listen to that voice, following its instructions more readily as you develop a strong sense of trust in it. Furthermore, this exercise will help you to distinguish between the inner voice of intuition and other random sound bites that come from your imagination or from your memory. The more time and effort you spend studying the "voices in your head", the easier it will become to tell them apart, allowing you to dismiss the junk and follow the advice of your intuition.

Finally, there is the method of strengthening your dreams. Again, keeping a journal is one of the best methods for achieving this goal. Each morning take the time to write down as much as you can remember about your dreams from the previous night. At first, you might not remember much, but as you continue the practice, you will discover your dream recall will improve exponentially. Furthermore, the intensity and frequency of your dreams will also increase, making your dreamtime that much more productive. Writing down your dreams will help you to discern the difference between those dreams that are simply fantasy-driven, as opposed to those that are, in fact, messages from your intuition. Soon you will know which dreams to listen to, and how to understand the message they are telling you. Again, it may start as a matter of trial and error where you understand the message a dream was sending after the fact. Eventually, you will begin to recognize the messages more readily, enabling you to follow them and enjoy the benefits they have to offer. This will also go a long way to developing all other clairvoyant capabilities as the development of dreams is, in essence, the development of the mind's eye.

If you still are unsure as to your inherent intuitive abilities, the best plan of attack is to try developing one at a time, taking about a month in each case. If you spend a month developing your dream recall but make little to no progress for a month, then maybe dreams aren't your thing. Try developing your inner voice next, and if that produces few to no results, then move on to clairsentience or claircognizance. In the end, everyone has a specific talent in the realm of intuitive abilities. Some may already have a good idea as to what that talent is, whereas others may have to take the time to discover it for themselves. The important thing is to remain patient and diligent, putting in the time and effort needed to achieve the results that will come as long as you stay the course.

Chapter 4: The Clairs: Clairvoyance, Clairaudience, Clairgustance, Claircognizance and Clairsentience

At the heart of all psychic abilities are five main skills or gifts. These are commonly known as the "clairs"; clairvoyance, clairaudience, clairgustance, claircognizance, and clairsentience. Most of these have already been discussed to a small degree, but this chapter will delve deeper into each, revealing their true role in the quest to discover and develop your psychic talents. Furthermore, real-life examples will be given, helping you to know whether or not you have had any experience in one or more of these areas. All in all, any psychic ability can be traced to one "clair" or another, meaning that anyone with any psychic talents can identify with at least one of the psychic abilities discussed in this chapter. Additionally, exercises and methods for development will be discussed, giving you the tools you need to raise your psychic abilities to the next level.

Clairvoyance

Of all the "clairs", the one that is probably best known to the average person is clairvoyance. Again, this is the ability to clearly see with the mind's eye, as is described by the name itself, which means "clear seeing". Although clairvoyance is a single term, there are numerous forms of clairvoyance, each unique in its own way. For example, some people can see events in other people's lives by tapping into their clairvoyant ability. This is where the image of a fortune teller using a crystal ball comes into play. While few clairvoyants actually use a crystal ball to harness their visions, the image itself is what is important. Such a person can see an image as clear as day in their mind, one that involves another person or group of people. These images can be warnings of impending danger or good omens pointing to job promotions, meeting a future spouse, or even the birth of a child. In the end, it is a bit like daydreaming about someone else's life—the only difference being that, in this case, the dream actually comes true.

Most people have experienced clairvoyance at least once in their life, whether or not they realize it. This is where the second form of clairvoyance comes into play, namely that of seeing a person in your mind that you will cross paths with in real life in the immediate future. Countless stories exist where a person sees an image of a friend or loved one, sometimes someone whom they haven't seen in a long time, only to get a phone call or surprise visit from that person during the day. A good example of this is a story where a store manager for a retail store always knew when the district manager would make a surprise visit because he would see his district manager's face either in a dream the previous night or in his mind's eye during the morning as he got ready for work. Needless to say, this gave him a huge advantage as he was always prepared before the "surprise" visit, making him look good in his boss' eyes.

Another form of clairvoyance is the ability to see a place or an event that you will come in contact with before the fact. Numerous accounts exist of people "seeing" their next house before deciding to look for another place to live. At first glance, this might not seem like an important ability; however, it can have very profound implications. While the mere fact that a person sees a house even before looking for it is amazing, the message beneath the phenomenon will, more often than not, be one of validation. In other words, knowing what your future house will look like can help you to make the right decision, turning down the other options until you find the one your intuition has prepared you for. The very same thing can happen in terms of choosing a new job, car, or even significant other. Any time you see the final outcome, you no longer have to guess at what decision to make. This ensures that you make the right decision every time.

Even so, while almost everyone has had a clairvoyant experience at one time or another, it doesn't mean that clairvoyance is everyone's personal psychic ability. The question, therefore, is how do you know if it is your personal ability? The simple answer comes down to two things: frequency and intensity. If you have had numerous experiences of seeing a person or event before it happens, even making it ordinary and mundane in your mind, then you have the knack of clairvoyance. Additionally, if your dreams are vivid, or you can imagine things in your mind with great clarity and detail, then clairvoyance is probably your gift. Once you make that determination, the next step is to develop your ability to the highest level possible.

The very first step to achieving this goal is to practice meditation regularly. You don't have to do anything elaborate; simply engage in a practice that enables you to clear your mind at the beginning and end of each day. Clearing your mind in the morning will help you to tap into your clairvoyance during the waking day, enabling you to see things before they unfold. Performing the practice at the end of the day will help you to dream better at night, giving you a clear mind that will be more open to vivid images from the spirit realm. Another proven technique for developing your clairvoyance is to keep a clairvoyant journal. In this journal, you will record all of your dreams, along with the images you receive during the regular day. Next to each vision, you will record the corresponding event that unfolds, reflecting the accuracy of your vision. The purpose of this exercise is twofold. First, it will create a sense of confidence in your ability, thereby causing you to pay more attention to the phenomenon as well as accepting the messages you are receiving. Second, it will increase your connection to your mind's eye. The more time you spend focusing on your experiences, the stronger and more frequent they will become. In the end, by ensuring that your mind is clear and by recording your visions as they occur, you will soon develop your clairvoyance to the point where you will see any event or outcome by simply tuning into your inner vision, thereby giving you an untold advantage when it comes to making the right choices and decisions every single time.

Clairaudience

The next clair to consider is that of clairaudience. As already mentioned, this is the ability to hear with the mind, hence the meaning of the name—"clear hearing". Although not as common as clairvoyance, this is another psychic phenomenon that many people all across the globe have experienced at one time or another. Simply put, this is when you hear something that could not be heard in the physical world around you. More often than not, such a sound will be a voice, usually telling you a word, number, or some other message as though someone was whispering in your ear. Unfortunately, most people dismiss such encounters as a trick of the wind or a mere figment of their imagination. Herein lies an important lesson, however. Even if such a voice were the product of a person's imagination, that does not mean that the message itself is inaccurate or unimportant. After all, what is imagination if not a form of inner dialogue? Therefore, the mechanics of clairaudience are not as important as the nature of the event itself. If you hear a voice, one that you know is not of your physical environment, you should listen to what it says regardless of its origin.

Another way that clairaudience takes shape is in the person behind the voice. Sometimes the message being conveyed isn't about the words being spoken; rather, it is about the person speaking them. Thus, if you ever thought you heard a person's voice, such as a friend or a loved one, even though that person is nowhere around, it could very well be that they are either thinking of you at that moment or in need of your help. Sometimes such an event can simply foretell of a chance encounter with that particular person later in the day, or even a phone call or email from them. The important thing to remember is that if you hear a voice that you recognize, even though that person is nowhere around, then that person is significant in the moment for one reason or another. It is up to you do discover that significance throughout the day. Whether you choose to call that person to check up on them or simply keep an eye out for them during the day, the important thing is never to dismiss such an event as you could miss out on a meaningful experience.

A good example of a real-life experience of clairaudience occurred at a funeral, where a well-loved husband and father was being laid to rest. Although the funeral took place without incident, it was after the event that things got interesting. A friend of the family had attended the funeral as a courtesy, even though he had never spent any time with the man who died. During the reception, he approached the daughter and asked what her dad called her mother, such as nicknames or the like. Dumbfounded by the question, the daughter didn't respond. At that point, the friend told her that he heard a voice at the gravesite say, "Hey, hun," as clear as day. His statement made the daughter tear up, as it turned out that it was exactly what her father called her mother all of the time.

When it comes to determining whether or not clairaudience is your skill set, the same elements apply as with clairvoyance. Namely, how often and how clearly do you hear voices? If you hear voices clearly and regularly, the chances are that you have a heightened ability when it comes to clairaudience. The next thing to do is to develop your skill set as much as possible. Fortunately, the same techniques used to develop and strengthen clairvoyance are the ones you will need for developing and strengthening clairaudience. First and foremost, you need to practice meditation regularly. After all, if your mind is filled with clutter and noise, you won't be able to hear much of anything beyond your own thoughts. However, when your mind is clear, you will hear with your inner ear just as well as you can with your physical ear. Next, you need to keep a journal in which you record every encounter. At first, some of your experiences may prove to be false readings—the consequence of the clutter filling your mind. However, after the practice of meditation begins to take hold and your focus on your inner ear increases, your encounters will become more frequent, more intense, and, most importantly, more accurate.

Clairgustance

Perhaps the least common of all the clair phenomena is that of clairgustance. Meaning "clear tasting", this is the ability to virtually taste something without having to have it in your mouth. This ability may appear completely useless at first glance—after all, what possible significance can a flavor have? However, truth be told, the sense of taste, along with smell, has been shown to be the chief senses responsible for triggering a person's memory. How many times have you eaten a piece of pie or some other home-made cooking only to recall early childhood memories of eating similar tasting foods? This doorway to the memory can be highly effective when it comes to connecting to friends or loved ones, near or far, alive or departed.

The notion that a departed soul continues to love and care for those they left behind is a common belief among countless traditions from every culture and every point in human history. Since physical speech is impossible for a departed soul, they must rely on another form of communication, one that will allow them to be seen or heard despite the veil that separates them from the living. Since taste can evoke some of the strongest memories, what better way to communicate than by putting a familiar taste in the mouth of the person they are trying to communicate with? Therefore, the next time you start tasting your long-departed grandmother's cookies, rather than simply dismissing it as a random fluke, take the time to contemplate your grandmother, even speaking to her, telling her how much you love and miss her. There is a real good chance that she is telling you the very same thing by sending you the taste of her cookies, thereby bringing her to mind.

The language of clairgustance isn't restricted to the departed. Instead, it can be just as effective when it comes to connecting to people who are still very much a part of the physical realm. If, for example, you begin to taste your mother's cooking, even though she is hundreds of miles away, it can be more than just a passing fancy—she may be thinking of you at that moment, causing you to react by experiencing a taste that brings her face to mind. Alternatively, she may need your help, or about to call or visit you. In the end, the language of taste is a bit vague in that it can't provide a clear context all of the time, such as clairvoyance or even clairaudience. Therefore, this is one skill set that really needs to be developed carefully if it is to be of any real value.

One way to improve your clairgustance ability is to keep a journal in which you record any flavors that occur seemingly out of the blue. Next to the flavor, write down the person or event that you associate it with. Finally, note any encounters that might explain the event in the first place. In other words, if you find yourself tasting your mother's food, then get a phone call or a visit from her later in the day, record those things together, allowing you to see the relationship between your psychic experience and your physical experience. If this is something you can't relate to at all, then the chances are that you don't have the knack for clairgustance. Since this is the rarest of the clair abilities, it wouldn't be surprising. However, if this is something you have experienced from time to time, then you might be one of the very few individuals who possess this ability, making it absolutely vital that you put in the time and energy needed to nurture and strengthen this rare and unique gift.

Claircognizance

Claircognizance, or "clear knowing", is probably one of the most useful of the clair abilities, enabling a person to virtually know a thing without ever having had experience or training in the area before. In fact, this is the ability that is most associated with the overall concept of intuition. One of the more commonly accepted definitions of intuition is that of an inherent knowledge—something that is understood from within rather than from without. Sometimes this knowledge comes in the form of inspiration or imagination, making a person appear to be a virtual genius with what they can produce or accomplish. Other times it comes in the form of timely knowledge, such as simply knowing to avoid a certain road at a certain time, only to find out later that an accident on that road could have proven devastating, both in terms of time and even wellbeing. In the end, the common thread is that claircognizance is the ability to know beyond what the physical senses can perceive. This gives a person untold insight into the world around them, enabling them to pursue levels of success few ever dream of.

There are many different ways in which claircognizance can manifest itself in a person's life. One way, albeit a less than desirable one, is that of a constant, nagging thought that won't go away. Sometimes this can appear as the proverbial "red flag" when you know that something just doesn't add up with regards to a situation or story. Although you can't put your finger on it at the moment, you know that there is more than meets the eye. This can often be confused with clairsentience, and the two often overlap, meaning that you might have a bad feeling about something because things don't add up. However, claircognizance goes the extra step further, enabling you to divine the answer in due course. Some refer to this as the process of germination, in which the seed of an idea virtually grows within the individual, eventually producing the solution to the problem at hand. The result is that "eureka moment" when you finally understand a particular situation, albeit from an intuitive perspective.

A good example of this is in the case of a liar. People with claircognizance will almost always be able to spot a liar because their intuition tells them there are problems with the story being told. Again, a bad feeling may accompany this event, bridging clairsentience with claircognizance; however, the claircognizant person will eventually be able to piece together the anomalies of the story, proving the false intentions of the person involved. Another way that claircognizance takes shape is through random and seemingly unrelated thoughts or ideas just coming to mind. This isn't the same thing as the random noise that fills most people's minds; instead, it is when a person has a random thought or idea that proves significant in the immediate future. Such things as cooking extra food, only to have unexpected guests arrive during dinner, or closing the windows before leaving your house on a sunny and cloudless day, counting your blessings when you watch heavy rains appear seemingly out of nowhere. Such knowledge of events beyond the horizon is a clear sign of claircognizant abilities.

It is fairly easy to determine whether or not you are one of the many people with this particular skill set. All claircognizant people tend to have a love for problem-solving, more often than not tapping into their intuition to find solutions others would never have thought of in a million years. Additionally, claircognizant people tend to analyze things carefully, giving them the insights needed to make the best decision every time. If you can relate to these traits, you are probably claircognizant. Furthermore, if you have ever done something or made a decision that seems out of place in the moment, but that proves highly correct and valuable later on, you most likely know how to tap into your intuition and follow its lead.

Developing claircognizance is a matter of trust more than anything else. Most people with this ability have clear thoughts already—the problem is that they don't always act on those thoughts, usually because there is no logical reason to. However, more often than not, those thoughts prove themselves to be true soon enough. Not closing the windows on that sunny and clear day, only to come home to a soaking windowsill, is just one example of when that inherent knowledge proves itself infallible. The best way to build that trust is to keep a diary, one in which you record the thoughts that you have, along with whether you followed your intuition or not. Then record the results. Unfortunately, there will be times when you won't be able to prove the value of following your intuition. After all, if you don't turn down a street, thereby avoiding an accident you would have been a part of, how will you ever know? Therefore, the biggest proof will usually come when you don't follow the intuition, resulting in the negative experiences that could have otherwise been avoided.

Clairsentience

The final clair to discuss is clairsentience, or "clear feeling". This is one of the easiest clair qualities to recognize and develop. Already discussed in fairly good detail in the previous chapter, clairsentience is the psychic ability to feel your way through a given situation. As with claircognizance, the feelings may tend to be bad rather than good, pointing to the purpose of the ability. All in all, most psychic abilities serve as warnings, helping to protect you from harm or from making decisions that you will later regret. Therefore, learning to recognize the times when you have episodes of clairsentience can go a long way to improving your day-to-day life by keeping you safe and on the path to success, avoiding the twists and turns that can lead you astray.

One of the easiest ways to determine whether or not you have the gift of clairsentience is to consider how you respond when meeting people for the first time. If you are easily taken in by fake people, then you probably don't have the gift. However, if you are the type who gets a "gut feeling" about a person, usually in stark contrast to their outward appearance, then this is probably your strong suit. Again, more often than not, the feeling will be negative, warning you of the underlying danger inherent in the person you are meeting or in contact with. Even if this person appears trustworthy and decent, if you have a bad feeling about them, that feeling will prove itself right sooner or later. When you ignore the feeling and trust what your physical senses are telling you, the chances are that you will pay the price for ignoring your intuition. However, when you follow your intuition, even when it seems completely wrong, you will be the one left standing when everything comes crashing down. If you are picturing the dozen or more times this has happened to you, then congratulations—you are a clairsentient!

Needless to say, gut feelings can be caused by intuition or what you had for lunch, or a lack of sleep or any other number of conditions that can affect your physical health and wellbeing. As such, you must always remain aware of the context of your feelings, recognizing whether or not there may be other explanations less sinister than deception or impending doom. Taking a step back anytime you have a gut feeling and contemplating its true nature will almost always yield immediate answers. After all, your intuition isn't out to fool you; instead, it is out to protect you. Therefore, if you have a bad feeling come out of nowhere and you take a moment to contemplate it, if it is the result of your lunch, your mind will tell you as much, one way or another.

However, if it is more significant, you can be sure your mind will alert you to the real danger at hand. After all, the feeling isn't the message itself; rather, it is the knock on the door or the ringing of the phone. It is only intended to get your attention. The trick is to recognize it when it does, to clear your mind and accept the first thing that comes to mind when you are in that state. You might have an image of a person or an event, or you might simply know that the feeling is related to a person you are with or an event you are currently engaged in. Taking the time to pay attention to any strange feelings you have, such as gut feelings, the hair on your neck or arms standing on end, symptoms of a panic attack for no logical reason, or any other physical anomaly that is out of step with the moment, is the first step to strengthening this skill set. The more in touch you become with your feelings, the stronger those feelings will become, and the more regular their occurrence.

The next step is to begin recording events in a journal. Only by studying your feelings and the circumstances that surround them can you begin to understand their origin and meaning better. This is also a really good way of being able to distinguish from intuitive feelings as opposed to those caused by physiological conditions. Furthermore, by recording the times that you had a bad feeling about someone, who later turned out to be a danger in one way or another, will enable you to trust your feelings more and more, thereby helping you to benefit from the message they are trying to send. In the end, the value of keeping a journal simply cannot be overstated. A person who keeps a journal never struggles with their psychic abilities. Alternatively, few people who don't keep journals ever enjoy the full potential of their inherent skills. So, if you want to develop your ability, no matter what it may be, the most important thing is to keep a journal in which you record events and then go back and review them afterward in order to learn the valuable lessons they contain.

Chapter 5: Telepathy

From the Greek meaning "far away perception", telepathy is the psychic gift that enables one person to perceive the thoughts and feelings of another. Also known as "mind-reading", this gift is a fairly common one, more often associated with people who share a close bond, such as siblings or spouses. The ability for one person to finish the sentence or thought of their partner is no coincidence, nor is it the result of the two people having similar opinions. Instead, it is a sign of two people virtually sharing the same thoughts. While couples can develop telepathic abilities together, usually limited to their own thoughts and feelings, it is also possible for an individual to develop those very same abilities, enabling them to pick up on the thoughts and feelings of the people around them as well as individuals far away. This chapter will explore the science behind telepathy, as well as various ways in which telepathic abilities can be nurtured and strengthened. Furthermore, real-life examples of telepathic communication will be revealed, helping you to know whether telepathy is your personal psychic gift.

Understanding the True Nature of Telepathy

The first thing to understand about telepathy is that it is not the ability to tap into someone else's mind and read their thoughts as though you were reading a page in a book. Had this been the case, the original Greek word would have been different, using the term for "reading" rather than "perceiving". Instead, the phenomenon is based on perception, or the ability to sense another person's thoughts. Sometimes this can come in the form of the other person's thoughts appearing as your own, while other times, the origin of the particular thought is more obvious. However, the result is always the same, namely that the thought becomes your thought as well. Therefore, in a nutshell, telepathy can be seen as the ability to share thoughts, both in terms of sending thoughts to others and receiving thoughts from others.

How those thoughts manifest differs from one person to the next, being determined on how the individual's mind functions. In the case of someone gifted in clairaudience, for example, another person's thoughts can come in the form of an inner voice speaking a word or phrase. Alternatively, someone more prone to visualization will see images, whether of people, colors, objects, or even events. When two people of similar mindsets share thoughts, the results can be clearer, such as clearer images in the case of two clairvoyants, or clearer sounds in the case of two clairaudients. Fortunately, both members don't have to have similar mental qualities; rather, it simply enhances the experience.

The Science Behind the Phenomenon

Studies on the human brain have revealed numerous insights when it comes to the phenomenon of telepathy. One such insight is that the mind is designed to receive signals from outside of the body as well as from within. Professor Gregor Domes performed tests in 2007, demonstrating that certain "cues" within social interactions can be picked up by a person, allowing them virtually to know the intentions of someone else. More often than not, this plays out in the arena of dating, where certain chemistry is formed between two people interested in starting a relationship. When one person is less willing that chemistry is lacking. Although the term "chemistry" has often been used casually to describe the nature of the connection, it turns out that the term is far more accurate than most people realize. In fact, the hormone oxytocin is the main element required for receiving these social cues, proving that the chemistry in the situation is very much real.

The long-distance nature of telepathy was put to the test in 2014 when psychiatrist Charles Grau ran tests to determine whether or not the internet could be used to enhance telepathic abilities. Experiments showed that people in India were able to communicate words such as "ciao" or "hola" to people as far away as Spain by just thinking of them while being online. They did not have to type the words, say the words, or use them in any other way. Just by thinking the words clearly in their minds, they could convey them across thousands of miles to the recipients at the other end. Although this experiment could be seen to prove that certain people are highly gifted with telepathic abilities, the true revelation was the significance of the internet itself. It seems that thoughts, just like any other form of communication, can be transmitted electronically. Thus, you can think of them as radio waves, moving from one person to another. And, just like radio waves, the best way to hear the message is to be on the same wavelength as the sender, literally tuning in to their mind.

Another study conducted in 2008 served to locate the very part of the brain connected to telepathic activity. Two test subjects, one adept at telepathy, otherwise known as a mentalist, and the other a control subject with no demonstrable telepathic skill sets, were asked to draw an image based on one that had been prepared in secret. While the mentalist produced a strikingly similar image, the control subject did not. Even more telling was the fact that the parahippocampal gyrus in the mentalist was activated during the experiment, whereas it was not activated within the control subject. This definitively proved the difference between true telepathy as opposed to sheer guesswork.

While the detailed studies of professional scientists can shed a great deal of light on the nature of telepathy, it only takes a basic understanding of science to realize how telepathy actually makes sense. Again, thoughts are known to be electrical signals, just like radio waves. It is also common knowledge that water is a good conductor of electricity. This is why it's not a good idea to stand in a puddle during a lightning storm. Since the human body is comprised of about 60 percent water, it stands to reason that a person's body can act as a prime conductor of electricity, and thus, a prime conductor of thoughts. While this would explain close proximity telepathic experiences, only true psychic ability can explain the long-distance examples, meaning that telepathy can be seen as both a natural and supernatural phenomenon.

Examples of Telepathic Experiences

One of the best examples of real-life telepathic experiences can actually be found within the animal kingdom. The simple truth is that telepathy is not merely a human ability; rather, numerous animals have been found to possess the ability as well. Birds are one such example. Any time you see a flock of birds flying in formation, you will notice that the entire group can virtually turn on a dime. Thus, when the lead bird changes direction, the whole flock does as well. Needless to say, this prevents mid-air collisions that would make flying in flocks dangerous and even deadly. The question is, how do the birds know when to change direction? Telepathic communication is the answer. This is an example of close proximity telepathy, in which an individual can ascertain the intention of another. The message travels from one bird to the next in split-second timing, creating a wave pattern when the flock changes direction.

Fortunately, there are countless examples of telepathic communication within the human species as well. Some of the most amazing examples come from accounts where twins shared a similar experience, albeit unknowingly at the time. One story involves a twin who cut their heel while shaving in the shower one day. A few days later, she noticed her twin had a bandage on her heel as well. It turns out that she had gotten her first tattoo on the exact spot and at the exact time that the other twin had cut herself in the shower. While this isn't "reading minds" per se, it demonstrates the true nature of telepathy, namely distant perception.

Another story involves twins who were still in school when they had their experience. One twin had to stay in class to take a test while the other went to get a blood test. During the test, the one boy noticed a broken blood vessel on his elbow. A few hours later, when the twins were reunited, he realized that his brother had a bandage on his elbow in the same place, the place where the needle had been injected for the blood test. Again, while this isn't about thinking the same thoughts, it is about sharing the same experience through telepathic communication. The thought process of the one was transmitted to the other, at which point the brain sent a signal to the body, causing a similar physiological reaction.

Numerous accounts exist telling of when a husband and wife send signals to each other, such as where one has an urge to stop for pizza on the way home, only to discover that the other had a craving for pizza, or where one picks up a gallon of milk not on the grocery list while at the store, only to discover that the other had spilled their milk at virtually the same moment. In the end, as compelling as these stories are, the fact remains that they are still stories, and thus they aren't as compelling as cut and dry scientific data. Fortunately, there is an undeniable trend in scientific data that demonstrates, if not outright proves, that telepathy is real. Countless experiments have been done where a person has had to guess things, such as the identity of someone sending a message or the picture on a card someone is holding, that have produced virtually the same results. When people with no telepathic abilities simply guessed at the answer, the average success rate was between twenty to twenty-five percent. Alternatively, when someone skilled in telepathy, such as a mentalist, underwent the same experiment, the success rate almost doubled, reaching as high as 43 percent. This undeniable evidence proves that telepathy is more than a gimmick; instead, it is a very real and observable phenomenon. Needless to say, if the stories mentioned earlier sound familiar, in that you have had similar experiences in your life, then it points to the fact that telepathy is your inherent psychic ability.

How to Develop your Telepathic Abilities

Many of the exercises needed to develop your telepathic abilities are the same as those needed to develop any other psychic ability. This is because the fundamental nature of all psychic abilities is largely the same, namely the ability to tap into your inner senses and understand the message those senses are telling you. Therefore, while some of the exercises listed below will seem redundant, it is only because of their absolute importance. Only when you earnestly practice such things as meditation and yoga regularly, if not daily, will your abilities begin to develop in any real and significant way. The following are a few exercises that will help you to harness and strengthen your telepathic abilities:

- **Meditation:** Again, to tap into your psychic abilities, you must gain control over your mind, specifically the amount of noise and clutter contained therein. Just as it becomes difficult to hear what another person is saying when you are in a noisy room, so too, it can be all but impossible to hear your inner voice when your mind is loud and full of chaos. Therefore, practicing relaxation meditation regularly is highly recommended, as this will help you to quiet your mind, thereby enabling you to develop a stronger connection to your inner voice. Additionally, mindfulness meditation is a good practice for developing your telepathic skill sets as this form of meditation is designed to strengthen your ability to focus on a single thought or idea, taking hold of it long enough to grasp its meaning thoroughly before letting go of it once again. For best results, it is recommended that you practice both forms together, starting with relaxation meditation to clear your mind and then moving on to mindfulness meditation to exercise your powers of perception.

  The last form of meditation needed to develop your telepathic skills is that of visualization. This form will help you to strengthen your ability to envision an object, person, event, or idea with greater clarity and conviction. Since only the strongest thoughts travel well, you must think clearly and soundly if you ever want to send your thoughts to another person. This is another way in which thoughts can be seen as being similar to radio waves. Weak radio transmissions only travel over short distances and are usually hard to hear over the other noise around. In contrast, strong radio signals can travel great distances, drowning out all unwanted noise, thereby capturing the attention of the listener. By developing your visualization abilities, you will ensure that the signal you send to others is strong, clear, and powerful, thus getting the desired message through every time. All of the steps for these forms of meditation are clearly outlined in the above chapter on meditation.

• **Yoga:** It is recommended that you practice yoga as well as relaxation meditation to clear your mind and achieve the relaxed state of being needed to connect with your inner psychic abilities. In addition to deepening the relaxed state of your mind, yoga has many physiological benefits that will help to improve your telepathic abilities. One such benefit is the improved blood flow to the brain. By stretching out your muscles, you will release the tension that can reduce the flow of blood carrying oxygen to your brain, thus improving your mental clarity. The more blood your brain receives, the more oxygen it gets. Oxygen is vital for such things as clarity of thought, memory, and the ability to visualize—this is fundamental for anyone trying to develop their telepathic communication. Yoga can be practiced in conjunction with meditation or practiced on its own. The important thing is to integrate yoga into your day-to-day life in order to give yourself the best chance of success in developing any psychic skill.

• **One-on-one practice:** Since telepathy requires a minimum of two participants, this is one of the psychic skills that you can develop with the help of another. While you can choose anyone to help you in this exercise, it is recommended that you pick someone who has, at the very least, an open enough mind to believe in telepathy, and at the most, some experience of their own concerning telepathic communication. If you pick someone who doesn't believe in the process, your results will be hampered. Once you find a suitable partner, the next step is to create some exercises that will help you to hone your telepathic skills. One of the best exercises is to play the time-tested game of "Which card am I holding?" Sit at a table facing one another and have your partner draw a random card from a deck of cards. Let them stare at the card for about ten seconds, focusing strongly on what they see. As they are staring at their card, take the time to clear your mind of all thoughts, keeping it open to receive their message. Next, take it one step at a time. Don't try to see the exact card at first; instead, try to see the color. You can ask them questions, leading you to the answer. If you see red in your mind, ask them if the card is red. Next, try to see if it is a number card or a face card. These are the most significant elements of the card, so they will be the bulk of the message. If you don't see a picture, such as that of a queen, king, or jack, ask if it's a number card. If they say "yes," then go on to narrow down the specific number and the specific suit. In the end, getting half of the elements right is a sign that you are doing more than merely guessing, so don't see that as a failure. Furthermore, as time progresses, you will see your results improve as your ability increases.

Another exercise using the same setting is to reverse the roles, allowing you to act as the sender. Have the other person try to hear your thoughts on the card you are holding. After all, this is the true nature of the exercise. You aren't trying to guess the card, nor are you trying to tap into mediumship or clairvoyance in order to read the card. Instead, you are trying to hear the message the other person is sending you—or in this case, send a message to the other person. Acting as the sender will help to strengthen your ability to visualize, which can help you to see the images another person is sending you. Therefore, use both roles regularly, taking the opportunity to develop your skills as both receiver and sender. This is particularly true if you struggle reading the messages being sent to you. By switching roles, you can give yourself a break while also strengthening the skills that will enable you to receive messages more clearly and accurately.

Chapter 6: Mediumship

Mediumship is one of the more complex forms of psychic ability, consisting of numerous variations, each entailing its own unique skill sets and results. Often confused with general psychic abilities, mediumship is one of the rarer gifts found within the psychic community. This is another example where although all mediums are psychics, not all psychics are mediums. Compared to all other forms of psychic practice, mediumship is the one that works more closely with the spirit realm. This is because the very nature of mediumship requires at least one spirit guide to perform any medium-oriented activities. This chapter will explore the fascinating field of mediumship, showing how it is distinct from general psychic abilities, as well as addressing the various forms that mediumship can take. Furthermore, it will discuss how you can know if you have the necessary skill sets for practicing mediumship, as well as several methods for honing and strengthening medium abilities.

Understanding the Differences between a Medium and a Psychic

One of the biggest misunderstandings about psychic abilities is that all psychics are somehow the same. In a way, it's a bit like saying all artists are the same. Needless to say, this is obviously untrue as anyone knows that art consists of a diverse range of forms, each unique and requiring specific skills and talents. For example, you wouldn't expect an artist who paints to be able to create a sculpture from a single block of stone. Nor would you give a sculptor a set of paints and tell them to create a masterpiece. While both are artists, their talents are very different, meaning that they are not interchangeable. Psychics are the same way. A medium is not necessarily a clairvoyant, nor is a telepath necessarily a medium.

As already discussed, a psychic is someone who has a strong set of internal senses, similar to the physical senses, but not requiring physical input. However, that is generally where the similarities end. From that point forward, each different form of psychic practice takes on its own shape and requirements, making it right only for a select number of people with psychic abilities. Mediumship is a prime example of this dynamic. Although the practice of mediumship draws on some of the general psychic abilities, specifically the five clairs, it has an added dimension that sets it apart from all other psychic disciplines. That dimension is the necessity of a spirit guide. Most other psychic activities can be performed by an individual without any help from another entity. In contrast, mediumship requires another entity, making this more of a relationship than merely a practice.

The nature of this relationship can best be explained in the name itself. Mediumship comes from the root word "medium", which is defined as a channel or mode of communication. Therefore, a person who is a medium acts as a virtual radio through which a spirit conveys a message. That isn't to say that all messages are verbal; rather, they can come in many different ways, including divination, automatic writing, smoke billets, and numerous other forms of communication. In the end, the most important thing to realize is that the medium is not the source of the message; they are merely the messenger, giving voice to a departed spirit, angel, or another entity who needs to communicate with a living person.

The Different Types of Mediumship

What makes mediumship so complex is that the various forms it takes are quite different, so much so that not all mediums are capable of practicing every form. Perhaps the most common form in terms of popular culture is physical mediumship. This is often portrayed in the movies or on TV, where a medium goes into a trance and can levitate a table, much like in most depictions of a séance. While the image portrayed in popular culture tends to treat the practice of physical mediumship as a mere gimmick or party trick, the truth is far different. Physical mediums engage in their practice daily, usually in ways that enable them to gain insights into current and important issues. Divination can be seen as an example of this practice. Although an individual can practice divination in theory, most have come to believe that a spirit guide is necessary to produce accurate readings. Therefore, it is the relationship between the spirit and the medium that enables an individual to draw the right Tarot card or cast the perfect rune. The trick is that the individual yields themselves to the spirit, surrendering their will and desire in order to allow the spirit to act through them. Only then can clear communication occur, no matter what form it takes.

Another form of mediumship is known as spiritual mediumship. This form relies heavily on the five clairs, using such things as a person's ability to see, hear, feel, and know with their inner senses alone. Although a medium may choose to enter a trance-like state to achieve their goal of getting an otherworldly message, this isn't always necessary. Instead, a person can simply clear their mind to make room for the message to enter. The important thing is that the medium can set aside their personal thoughts and feelings in order to allow the message from the spirit to enter their mindfully and clearly. This is one of the main reasons why mediumship is rarer than many other forms of psychic activity. The highest level of clarity and control is needed to communicate effectively with spirits, thus requiring someone with highly advanced skills for this practice.

Before moving on to the other two forms of mediumship, it should be noted that physical and spiritual mediumship have many similarities, making them equally suited for someone with the inherent talents of mediumship. One similarity is that departed souls are often the spirit contacted for communication. Again, the iconic séance is a prime example of this activity. Whenever a person wants to contact a departed loved one, they can call on a medium to act as a bridge, conveying the message of the living person to the departed, and similarly transmitting any message that the departed soul might like to send as a response. The message from the spirit may come in the form of spoken words, an image, or even a written message in the form of automatic writing, also known as psychography, literally "psychic writing".

The next type of mediumship to explore is healing mediumship. This often comes in the form of a person laying their hands on a sick or troubled individual, thereby sending healing energy to the individual, enabling them to recover from their affliction. While this may seem like general psychic healing, the main difference is that the practitioner relies on another spirit or entity to act as the source of the energy. Thus, it isn't just the energy of the medium at work; rather, it is the energy of a spirit guide, an angel, or the Universe itself that travels through the medium and into the afflicted person. This phenomenon can be seen in many shamanic traditions where a medicine man or a healer channels supernatural energies through their body in order to heal a person—or in some cases, cast out a dark or malevolent spirit. Voodoo is another tradition that sees this practice performed regularly.

The final type of mediumship to examine is channeling mediumship. In a way, this is just like the other forms already discussed where a person channels messages, energies, or some other element to or from spirits of one form or another. However, the main difference here is that the spirit or spirits contacted are limited to only a select few. In other words, a channeling medium only communicates with specific spirits, much like a prophet communicating with a higher power. This means that such a medium would be ill-suited for performing a séance as the spirits in question there would not necessarily be the ones they have been chosen by to act as a medium for. Instead, channeling mediums are more often than not self-professed messengers of specific entities. These entities are often higher beings, such as angels or even the Supreme Deity.

Alternatively, they may be entities from another dimension or realm of existence. In the end, channeling mediums are chosen by their spirit guides to perform specific functions or give specific messages. This is probably the rarest form of mediumship and the one that most people dismiss as a hoax simply because they cannot always verify the information being presented.

Some Real-Life Examples of Mediumship

Rather than providing specific examples of messages conveyed through mediumship, it would probably be more impactful to provide examples of real-life mediums, many of which you have probably already heard of but never identified as mediums. One of the best examples of a modern-day medium is Edgar Cayce. Although he referred to himself as a clairvoyant, this doesn't take away from the fact that the nature of his abilities points to him being a skilled medium. The main reason for this was the fact that he always found his messages in dreams. This reflects the trance-like state that most mediums rely on to remove their personal thoughts and desires, thereby making them more open to receiving messages from the spirit world. Also known as the "sleeping prophet", it was his religious convictions that also lend credence to his being a medium rather than merely a clairvoyant.

Another group of people to consider when it comes to real-life mediumship is prophets. Whether they are the prophets of the Old Testament, the Prophet Mohammed, or any other individual claiming to speak on behalf of God or another deity, the simple truth is that the dynamic of such communication is nothing other than mediumship. Prophets are a good example of channeling mediums, chosen to transmit messages from specific spirits and those spirits alone. Many times these people were uneducated, being picked seemingly at random to perform the task at hand. Moses himself could be considered a medium as he acted as the mouthpiece of God in the Exodus account. Regardless of whether or not you subscribe to a particular religious belief, these individuals still embody the true nature of mediumship, namely the ability to act as a bridge between the spirit world and the physical world, along which messages of varying types can flow both ways.

If scientific proof is more your speed for understanding the reality of mediumship, then the next example is ideal for you. A study in Brazil using ten test subjects was conducted to determine whether or not there was any change in brain activity during the practice of psychography, or automatic writing. Five of the subjects had been practicing for many years, whereas the other five were relative newcomers to the field. Each subject was injected with a dye that would enable brain activity to be monitored. While every subject produced a psychographic document, not all the results were the same. Those more advanced in the field showed a significant decrease in activity in the area of the brain used for focus, planning, reasoning, and the like, namely the frontal lobe regions of the brain, as compared to when they wrote ordinarily, using their own thoughts and intellect. In contrast, the newcomers demonstrated higher levels of activity in these areas, indicating an increase in focus on their part.

Despite the difference in brain activity, the one thing all ten participants shared in common was the fact that their psychographic writings were all more complex in substance and nature than their ordinary writings, something the researchers simply could not explain. According to the scientists, the ordinary writings should have been more complex as they were given the most conscious attention and focus. The fact that all ten were able to baffle researchers in this way proved that psychography is more than a hoax. Instead, it is a real phenomenon, one that proves demonstrably that something out of the ordinary truly does occur in this form of mediumship. Furthermore, the five advanced mediums should have shown far less clarity and complexity in their writings as their focus and reasoning were significantly diminished, much like it would have been after several alcoholic drinks. Inexplicably, theirs were the most complex and intelligent writings, suggesting that they truly did channel communications from the spirit realm.

Is Mediumship Right For You?

The next question to tackle is whether or not mediumship is right for you. Fortunately, there are a few telling signs when it comes to identifying a natural-born medium. One such sign is the ability to feel changes within the energy of a given area. You might feel a sudden drop in temperature or a change in the "density" of the air for no apparent reason. If this happens to you regularly, it could indicate your ability to sense spirits that are present. Furthermore, if you get images or hear messages at the same time that you sense a change in the environment, this clearly suggests that not only can you sense spirits, but you can also communicate with them easily and naturally.

Another sign you might be a medium is if you see things out of the corner of your eye. More often than not, such peripheral activities are often dismissed as a trick of the eye or shadows and the like. However, it is also possible that these occurrences are a sign that you can recognize spiritual activity in your environment. The bottom line is that any change in energy will produce a visible anomaly, one that may be too subtle for your eyes to see when focused on the area in question—much like a faint star that can only be seen by shifting your focus to the left or right of it. However, peripheral vision can often detect such anomalies as the mind is less focused on filtering the incoming signals from those parts of the eye. Therefore, if you see movement out of the corner of your eye, even when there is nothing physically there, you might be seeing the energies of the spirits around you.

Hearing messages that later turn out to be true is another telltale sign that you have mediumship capabilities. Although clairaudience is not always the result of spirit guides or entities, it can be one of the main ways a spirit chooses to communicate with a medium. This is because hearing is the second strongest sense when it comes to receiving information. Since spirits cannot be seen with the physical eye, the mind is more open to hearing a spirit, and as a result, enables a medium virtually to hear the message being delivered. Therefore, before you start thinking you have lost your mind because you hear things or see things out of the corner of your eye, consider the very real possibility that you might be a natural-born medium.

How to Develop your Mediumship Skills

If you feel that mediumship is your form of psychic ability, then the next step is to hone and strengthen your mediumship skills. Fortunately, there are several simple and proven methods for achieving this goal, each of which can be implemented into your day-to-day life quickly and easily. One of the most important methods is to engage in the practices that enable you to have a clear mind at any time. Meditation and yoga are the two main exercises that will help you to master clarity of mind; therefore, you should practice these regularly if not daily.

Another good practice is to create a ritual that helps you to get into the mood and also that enables you to close the door when you are done communicating with the spirit world. This ritual can take any form whatsoever, so be creative and expressive, choosing the setting, the activities, and the words that work best for you. For example, you might choose to burn some incense in order to focus your mind on the present moment while praying to the spirits to help you hear and understand their message to you. After your session, you can extinguish your incense and begin mindfulness meditation, helping you to focus on your physical surroundings once again.

Perhaps the most important step toward improving your mediumship skills is to practice communicating with your spirit guides. It goes without saying that any medium will have at least one spirit guide specific to them—a guardian angel, so to speak. Begin chatting with your spirit guide in the way you would a regular person. Tell them things that are on your mind, both good and bad. Begin asking for help sorting out issues, then listen for the inspiration they provide. If you are a natural-born medium, you will instantly see the results—hearing inspired words, seeing images, and knowing information as soon as you ask your question or voice your concern. Communication with your spirit guide doesn't always have to be about work; instead, you can simply chat with them, asking such things as what they look like—if they ever had a physical form. Asking their name is another excellent way to establish communication with your spirit guide. Once you hear their name, use it when talking to them, as this will help strengthen your bond. One word of warning, however; try to limit your verbal communication to times when you know you will be alone—unless you are fine with other people thinking you have lost your mind. As time progresses, you will internalize your conversations, thereby enabling you to talk to your spirit guide anywhere, anytime.

Chapter 7: Psychometry

The next psychic ability to explore is psychometry. This is the ability to ascertain specific information about an object just by holding it. In other words, someone with psychometric skills can hold a coin or piece of paper currency and see where that coin or banknote has been in the past. Needless to say, this ability is not restricted to money; instead, it can be performed with any item at all, including articles of clothing, pieces of furniture, and even houses or other buildings in general. The basic premise behind this ability is that an item absorbs a certain amount of energy from every person and event that it encounters, much like a thumbprint. Therefore, it has a memory of that person or event, and someone with psychometric abilities can tap into that memory, thereby catching a glimpse of the past, albeit recent or far back into ancient history. This chapter will discuss the specifics of psychometry, including its uses, whether or not it is the right psychic ability for you, and ways to harness and strengthen any psychometric abilities you might have. When you have finished reading this chapter, you will know whether or not psychometry is your inherent psychic ability.

What is Psychometry?

The word psychometry is Ancient Greek and roughly translates as "soul measure". This definition can have two different meanings. On the one hand, the "psych" portion of the word can refer to the fact that psychometry is a psychic gift, one that is performed with your inner senses as opposed to your five physical senses. However, on the other hand, it can also indicate that what you are measuring is the energy of the object itself. This, in essence, suggests that you are tapping into the very soul of a particular object or place, much like telepathy is tapping into the mind of another person. Whether you believe that objects have souls or they simply accumulate residual energy is of little consequence. The bottom line is that a person with psychometric abilities can read the energy an object contains.

Again, a good way to envision this is to imagine that every person that touches an object leaves a small amount of their energy on that object, much like they leave behind their fingerprints when touching that object. And, just as fingerprints can be used to identify a person, so too can the residual energy left behind on an object. This is particularly true in the case of an object that is used by the same person regularly. Something like a hairbrush, wallet, or pair of glasses can contain a huge amount of residual energy from a single individual, making it easy for someone with psychometric skills to get a clear image of who that person is/was. Furthermore, items associated with specific events, such as sporting equipment or military equipment, can possess the energy of an event, allowing a psychometric expert to see a touchdown being scored just by holding the game's winning ball.

Perhaps a better way to imagine it is to think of the residual energy as a snapshot, a single image reflecting where that object has been. Someone with psychometric skills can literally read the images contained in an object, thereby seeing the history of the object. This is where things can get a bit dangerous though. For example, weapons such as bayonets or swords may contain the image of the brutal slaying of an enemy combatant. Likewise, buildings such as hospitals or prisons may contain residual energy of a negative nature, making for bad reading when it comes to the images presented. Therefore, it is always vital to choose the objects you will read with great care as the images they contain can be anything at all—from the most wonderful to the most horrifying. Additionally, it is commonly accepted that the more intense a situation is, the more energy that situation creates. Therefore, items may have clearer images of more negative events as those are usually the ones that create the most intense energy. This makes it all the more important to choose the objects you read with great care.

How You Can Tell if Psychometry is Right for You

When it comes to determining whether or not you have psychometric skills, this too can be an exercise fairly negative in nature. The reason for this is that most of the telltale signs of psychometric abilities are stressful and unpleasant, often causing a person great distress. One such example is if you feel overwhelmed or oppressed whenever you are in an antique store. While many people can spend hours looking at all the wonderful and mysterious relics from the past, anyone with psychometric abilities will tend to become depressed and even anxious in such a place. This is because all of the residual energy in the objects present will overwhelm their senses, much like hundreds of radios being turned on at once. Therefore, if you feel uncomfortable whenever you are around old items, especially in the case of being in an antique store or a thrift shop, then you are probably a good fit for psychometry.

Another way to know if you possess psychometry skills is if you feel heavy or sad in older buildings. Again, places such as hospitals, prisons, or any other place where the energy would be highly negative will doubtlessly have an impact on almost any psychic, even those without inherent psychometric talents or skills. However, if ordinary places such as old houses, railway stations, or even old buildings turned into restaurants cause you depression, fatigue, or even anxiety, then you are probably someone with natural psychometric abilities. Not being comfortable in second-hand clothing, using old furniture, and other such issues with anything that has been used before is almost always a clear sign of psychometric abilities.

The feelings you get from old places, or old objects, don't always have to be negative, however, to indicate psychometric skills. This comes down to the simple fact that empathy is at the heart of psychometry. Thus, when an empath can control the flow of information coming in, they can avoid the negative impact of such places as antique stores and the like. This is because they don't become overwhelmed by the energy surrounding them. As a result, rather than becoming stressed or fatigued, they can simply feel the energy around them, much like hearing the ambient sound of numerous conversations in a restaurant. Therefore, if old places feel different to you, or old objects have a quality that sets them apart from new ones, psychometry is probably right for you.

Real-life Applications of Psychometry

As with any other psychic ability, psychometry can have some very useful real-life applications. That said, those applications will be far fewer than the ones associated with a talent, such as telepathy, where real-time information can be obtained, helping a person make the best decisions and choices every time. Nevertheless, psychometry can prove more useful than a mere talking point at parties. One way that psychometry can be put to use is in the area of antiques themselves. Forgeries and fakes are commonplace in the antique market, providing a lucrative business for those who can pass off such fakes to would-be buyers. However, a person with psychometric abilities will be able to tell the difference between a real antique and a fake just by the energy signature of the item. No matter how old an object looks, if it is relatively new, it will lack the depth of energy that a true antique possesses. Even the most novice practitioner of psychometry can tell a new item from an old item just by holding it for a few seconds.

Another application, perhaps one more likely to occur in day-to-day life, is in the area of identifying the owner of lost objects. While a lost purse or wallet will usually contain a photo ID of the owner, things like keys, a phone, or a jacket won't. This means it can be all but impossible to know whom to look for if you spot a set of keys laying on a picnic table or chair in a restaurant. However, if you have psychometric abilities, you will hold that item for a moment and catch a glimpse of the person it belongs to. At the very least, you will know if it is a man or a woman, someone old or young, and hopefully, you will even be able to see the color of their hair. This can make all the difference when searching the nearby crowd to see whom the keys might belong to. Needless to say, when you see someone matching the image in your mind looking around as though they lost something, you can be sure they will appreciate you returning their keys or phone to them.

Equally as important as knowing how psychometry can be used in real life, so too, you must know its limitations. Unfortunately, television and movies often depict psychometry in a very unreal and irrational way. This is particularly true in any situation where a telepath holds a murder weapon in order to identify the murderer. There are several things wrong with this depiction, not least of which is the fact that no law enforcement agency would ever base an investigation on such a tip. Furthermore, this idea significantly underestimates the impact of the images that a telepath can see from an item. Not only would images from a murder weapon be devastating to your heart and mind, but the energy itself, full of horror and pain, would be immeasurably traumatizing. Therefore, no sane person would ever willingly use their psychometric skills in conjunction with a murder weapon, a torture device, or any other object knowingly used to create pain and suffering on another living being.

How to Develop your Psychometric Skills

As with any skill or talent, the best way to improve your psychometric skills is with practice, practice, and even more practice. Fortunately, the process for conducting a psychometric reading is very straight forward, requiring only five steps to accomplish. This means that you can practice virtually anytime, anywhere, and as often as you like. The following are the basic steps of a psychometric reading:

- *Step one:* Wash and dry your hands thoroughly before handling an object. This will remove any dirt that might interfere with the reading, as well as any residual energy left from handling a previous object. If you can't wash your hands, simply wipe them a few times on your pants leg, just enough to brush off any surface residue.
- *Step two:* Rub your hands together vigorously for about ten seconds. This will generate energy in your palms and fingertips. The more energy you have in your hands, the easier it will be to absorb energy from the object. A good way to know if you are ready is to hold your hands together after rubbing, slowly separating them to about a quarter of an inch apart. If you can feel a tingling sensation or a resistance to pulling them apart, you know you have generated the energy you need. If you don't feel anything, rub them for another ten seconds and try again.
- *Step three:* Pick up an object and hold it in your hands. If you are a beginner, it is recommended that you start with an object that would have been used daily, such as glasses, a hairbrush, or a set of keys. Not knowing the owner can also be useful as it will prevent your mind from conjuring up memories of the person, such as a friend or a loved one. This will ensure that any images you see are the result of the object and not your memory or imagination.
- *Step four:* Close your eyes and relax. Imagine you are waiting for the object to speak to you. Listen to what it is saying, clearing your mind, and focusing on anything you see or hear. Let the object do the talking. The quieter your mind, the better your chances will be of having a successful reading. You might want to take a couple of deep breaths first just to help you relax and clear your mind, bringing your attention to the moment at hand.
- *Step five:* Be receptive. One mistake beginners often make is rejecting images they think don't make sense. Remember, you have no idea where this object has been, so take the

images you see as fact. Furthermore, always grab on to the first image that comes to mind. This will be the most accurate as your mind hasn't had a chance to judge that image or alter it in any way. As you practice, you will develop a more receptive mind, one that accepts whatever it sees and hears without doubt or hesitation. Then you will be able to perform this task with greater confidence in the results you get, enabling you to see glimpses into the past wherever you go simply by opening your mind and allowing the objects to tell their story.

At first, your results may be random, at best, being about half accurate and half inaccurate. However, as you continue to practice, you will find that your accuracy levels will rise, eventually reaching as high as 85 to 90 percent, as is often the result with highly adept individuals when tested under laboratory conditions. Perhaps the most important thing to remember is that the ability of psychometry is to be enjoyed, so make it fun for yourself. Who knows, eventually you may be able to touch an old building and get a snapshot of what the town looked like 100 or even 200 years ago. You might even see the people who were present at the time. If you get good enough, you might even be able to hear what they were saying. After all, you will be one of the lucky ones who will know what it's like when the walls can actually talk!

Chapter 8: Aura Reading

One of the most hotly debated topics within the psychic community, as well as within the scientific community, is that of auras. Mystics and spiritual traditions have promoted the existence of auras for millennia, covering just about every culture across the globe. Despite the widespread belief in auras, many still dismiss their existence because most people cannot see them. Recent scientific studies have revealed that auras can, in fact, exist, giving credence to the ancient traditions. However, despite their findings, many scientists still debate the nature of auras and the significance they hold. Regardless of this ongoing debate, many people crave the ability to see and interpret the auras of people around them. This chapter will provide the tools needed for seeing auras, as well as insights regarding the true nature of auras and the meaning behind the different forms and colors they can take. Additionally, the role that chakras play concerning auras will also be discussed, along with how to read and interpret the color of each different chakra.

A Basic Overview of Auras

In most spiritual traditions, the nature and appearance of auras are largely the same. A person's aura is the energy that surrounds their body, forming a sort of envelope or bubble of pulsating, glowing energy that reflects their physical, emotional, and mental state of being. Sick people, for example, will have darker, less vibrant auras, some of which even seem incomplete with holes or areas missing. In contrast, healthy, happy people will have brighter auras, usually yellow or white, extending as far as three or four feet from their body, creating a virtual bubble of energy that shields them from negative energy in their surroundings.

Although the basic elements of an aura are largely agreed upon in terms of their size, their vibrancy, and the impact of positive and negative forces upon them, there are a few debates within psychic circles regarding the meaning of their colors. Some schools of thought claim that auras can contain the same colors as chakras with each meaning something similar if not exactly the same as their chakra counterpart. However, other traditions hold that there are fewer colors and that these colors hold a completely different meaning. A perfect example is the color red. While some traditions claim that red indicates sexuality, assertiveness, and a competitive nature, others suggest that it reflects anger or high levels of stress. Subsequently, context is all-important when it comes to interpreting the colors of auras as red may indicate that the individual is strong-willed, or rage-driven, and thus should be kept at a safe distance.

As already mentioned, numerous scientific studies have concluded that auras do, in fact, exist. However, these studies do little to support the idea that different colors represent different psychic abilities or spiritual qualities. Instead, the basic belief within the scientific community is that auras are nothing more than the electromagnetic field surrounding a living being. This is what is referred to as the Bio-Energetic Field within the scientific community. The different functions of the human body, such as circulation, digestion, and respiration, all create electrical impulses that travel throughout the body. Furthermore, these impulses create electrochemical reactions throughout the nervous system. Subsequently, when a person is in peak health, where all of these functions are operating at their highest levels, then there is a tremendous amount of electrical activity taking place all through the body, creating a halo effect around the individual. The healthier and more vibrant the individual is the brighter their bio-energetic field.

When a person is ill or has suffered trauma, this field is reduced, both in size and intensity.

While science believes that an aura is largely one layer of energy produced by the electrochemical activities within the body, certain spiritual traditions believe that there are as many as seven separate layers of an aura, each representing a unique quality or condition of the individual. These seven layers of the aura are as follows:

- *Layer one: Etheric.* This layer is the one closest to the body and is usually the easiest to see. Associated with the root chakra, it represents a person's physical health and wellbeing and is bright blue when the individual is in good health. Physically active people tend to have the brightest etheric layers.
- *Layer two: Emotional.* The emotional layer surrounds the etheric layer and is connected to a person's emotional wellbeing. Associated with the solar plexus chakra, it can be any color in appearance—the brighter the color, the healthier the person. When the colors are dark or muted, it represents stress, fatigue, or generally poor emotional health.
- *Layer three: Mental.* The mental layer is the third from the body and is associated with a person's mental health and wellbeing. Associated with the sacral chakra, this layer is bright yellow when in good health. Due to the mental nature of this level, it is easiest to see around the head and neck area and is most vibrant in creative people and intellects.
- *Layer four: Astral.* This level is the fourth from the body and is associated with the heart chakra. Representing the interpersonal relationships of an individual, it is pink or rosy red, most vibrant among those with loving personalities, whereas it can be subtle or even absent in introverts or those suffering heartbreak or depression.
- *Layer five: Etheric Double.* The etheric double layer is associated with the throat chakra and is the layer that represents your true self. This is another layer that can

contain any color, depending on the qualities of the individual. When a person is living a life per their true nature, this level will be most vibrant; however, someone who is disconnected from their true identity will have a muted fifth layer.

- *Layer six: Celestial.* Representing unconditional love and connection with all living things, this level is pearl-white and associated with the third eye chakra. Psychics and other spiritually-minded individuals display strong celestial layers.

- *Layer seven: Ketheric Template.* As the last layer, this is the one furthest from a person's physical body, reaching an estimated three feet. Associated with the crown chakra, this layer is gold in color and has the highest frequency vibration. It is considered the embodiment of a person's immortal soul; thus, it reflects the wellbeing of the individual across all incarnations. It also reflects the strength of a person's connection to the divine source.

Interpreting the Different Colors

As already mentioned, there are two main schools regarding the different colors of the aura and their meaning. For this book, the more common interpretation will be used, specifically that associated with the colors of the chakras. The following are the colors of the aura and their meanings:

- **Dark red:** Someone with a dark red aura will generally be hardworking, energetic, and active.

- **Bright red:** A bright red aura points to someone who has a highly competitive spirit, strives to win at whatever they do and is usually sexually assertive, harnessing raw, primal energy.

- **Orange:** A person with an orange aura is usually very business-minded, capable of handling facts and figures, as well as being good with people. They can also prove adventurous in nature, such as an entrepreneur.

- **Bright orange/yellow-orange:** This color points to someone with an academic nature, given to logic and deep thinking.
- **Yellow:** As the color might suggest, a yellow aura represents someone bright and sunny in disposition, spontaneous and expressive.
- **Bright Green:** People with bright green auras are generally social, given to community activities and occupations, such as teaching or daycare.
- **Dark Green:** A dark green aura suggests someone who is good at organizing and being goal-oriented.
- **Blue:** This color signifies a person who is sensitive to others and is a loyal and caring friend.
- **Indigo:** A person with an indigo aura is usually more introverted, preferring solitude and tranquility. As a result, they are usually calm and clearheaded, often showing artistic qualities.
- **Violet**: A violet aura can be found in people who are charismatic, often with a sensual personality, and who can easily make connections with others.
- **Lavender:** Highly sensitive, even to the point of being fragile, lavender aura people are very imaginative and in touch with higher levels of consciousness.
- **White:** This is the highest color, representing transcendence, spirituality, and a unity of body and mind.

One of the main things to look for, in addition to the color itself, is the brightness of the aura. When a person is healthy, happy, and in tune with their inner, true nature, their aura will be brighter and more vibrant. In contrast, someone who is depressed, ill, or suffering inner conflict will have a muted aura, sometimes even brown, representing the dark, dreary condition of their energy.

Chakras and Cleansing Techniques

Although chakras are separate from auras, they are closely related, influencing the strength and clarity of the aura itself. When chakras are balanced and unblocked, flowing naturally and strongly, a person's aura will be more vibrant and balanced. Alternatively, when chakras are blocked or out of balance, the aura will suffer, becoming smaller and more muted in appearance. Fortunately, by understanding chakras, their meanings, and how to manage them, you will maintain good chakra health, thus promoting a strong and healthy aura. The following is a list of the seven chakras, revealing their significance and the location of each within the physical body:

- Root Chakra: This is the lowest of the seven chakras, located at the base of the spine. Its color is red, and it represents being down to earth, raw energy, and physical activity.
- Sacral Chakra: The second of the chakras, located just below the navel, is orange. It is associated with creativity and procreation, giving life in all forms.
- Solar Plexus Chakra: Yellow in color, this chakra represents a person's ability to assimilate to new conditions. It also points to motivation and being goal-oriented. Located in the stomach region, it also affects healthy digestion.
- Heart Chakra: Located in the center of the chest, this chakra is green and represents love, relationships, and the awareness of one's soul.
- Throat Chakra: As the name suggests, this chakra is located in the base of the throat. Blue in color, it affects communication, specifically verbal communication.
- Third Eye Chakra: The most commonly known of all chakras, the third eye chakra is located in the forehead, just above the level of the physical eyes. Indigo in color, this chakra represents intuition and insight.
- Crown Chakra: The last and highest of the chakras, the crown chakra is associated with peace, wisdom, and

spirituality. Violet in color, it is located at the top of the head, just above the crown.

When balanced, each of the seven chakras serves to create, attract, or direct energy to different parts of the body. However, even when balanced and healthy, some chakras will tend to be stronger and more pronounced within an individual, creating specific characteristics that define the person. Someone with a strong throat chakra, for example, will be more adept at giving speeches or just verbal communication in general. The extra strong nature of the throat chakra may affect the overall color of their aura, giving it a blue hue reflecting the nature of the energy itself.

Keeping the chakras balanced and unblocked is a critical step toward maintaining good chakra health as well as good mental, emotional, and even physical health. Fortunately, there are a few simple techniques for ensuring that the chakras operate at peak efficiency, providing the energy needed to keep you at your physical and spiritual best. The techniques can be broken down into physical and non-physical, each providing a different approach to maintaining optimum chakra health.

Yoga is by far the most effective physical technique for keeping chakras open and strong. The act of stretching the body ensures that energy flows throughout unimpeded, thus increasing the health and wellbeing of all chakras and the functions they support. The relaxation element of yoga also helps reduce stress, making yoga a bit of a hybrid, combining the physical and non-physical elements into a single regimen.

Maintaining a proper diet is another physical technique for increasing chakra health. Processed foods, fried foods, and anything high in sugar content will make the body sluggish, filling it with toxins that impact the health of the chakras. Alternatively, fresh fruits, vegetables, and other healthy foods serve to provide energy to the body while cleansing it of toxins and other harmful elements. The result is greater chakra health, resulting in a more vibrant aura.

Meditation is one of the non-physical techniques to help improve chakra health. Although meditation can be a physical act, it is the mental aspect of it that affects chakra health and wellbeing. In short, the reduction of stress helps open chakras, allowing energy to flow naturally and in high quantities. The better your energy flow, the better your physical and emotional health and wellbeing. Therefore, if you want to improve the performance of your chakras, make sure to make meditation a part of your regular routine.

Finally, avoiding stress in any way possible is the key to maintaining good, strong chakra health. Taking the time to sit in a peaceful, tranquil environment regularly will go a long way to preventing the buildup of stress that can block and even shut down chakras, creating a seriously negative impact on your energy. Additionally, avoiding stressful situations can go a long way to protecting your chakras from the harm that stress can cause. In the end, all of the things that help to create and maintain a healthy state of mind will also help to create and maintain the best levels of chakra health.

How to Develop your Ability to Read Auras

Now that you know what auras are, what their colors mean, and the impact that chakras have on them, the final step is to develop your ability to read auras. As with all other psychic abilities, reading auras may not be right for everyone. In theory, any person can develop any psychic ability, at least to some level. However, the best approach is to discover the ability that is inherent to you and develop that to its greatest potential. The very same thing holds true for reading auras. If you aren't a natural in this particular skill set, you may find success elusive.

Fortunately, it is fairly easy to know whether you have the potential to read auras. One sign that you are gifted in this area is the ability to feel another person's energy. If you can't feel someone else's energy, the chances are that you will never be able to see it. It's all a matter of sensitivity. Thus, if you feel uneasy around someone who is a threat, or you feel at peace around someone who can be trusted, then you can clearly sense their energy. With practice, you should be able to translate the ability to feel energy into the ability to see energy.

Another signal that you might have the ability to see auras is if you often see things in your peripheral vision. This has already been discussed in reference to sensing spirits that are present. If you see shadows, motions, or other anomalies out of the corner of your eye, even when nothing is there, you will probably have an easy time seeing auras. The main reason for this is that auras are often best seen out of the periphery where the mind can't filter them out. Additionally, the subtle nature of auras can make them hard to see a face on them, much like a faint star in the night sky. If you relate to one or all of these skill sets, then practicing the following techniques for reading auras should enable you to have your first experience in no time.

The first step to reading auras is to develop your sense of clairsentience. This is when you feel the energy of the people around you. Start to pay close attention to how you feel when you are around certain people. If you feel uncomfortable around someone, take the time to see if they are angry or just negative in general. This doesn't necessarily mean that the individual is a bad person; rather, it can indicate that they are simply in a bad mood. Alternatively, if you feel good around someone, such as happy or safe, take the time to see what mood they are in to confirm your feelings. The more accurate your clairsentience is, the easier it will be to see auras.

The next step is to develop your peripheral vision. A good way to do this is to focus on a single point in the room for about a minute. Allow your eyes to go slightly out of focus so that you don't strain them by staring at one thing for too long. Once you have softened your focus, start observing the objects or people outside your direct line of sight. See how much detail you can make out while keeping your eyes fixed on the one spot. This will sharpen your ability to recognize things out of your normal range of view. As mentioned before, auras can usually be more easily seen when not focused on directly, so developing a strong peripheral vision is critical for reading auras.

Sensing color is the next step in developing the ability to see and read auras. This can be done by placing sheets of colored paper on a wall. The colors should represent the colors of the aura, or chakras, as you want to focus specifically on being able to see those more than any colors in general. Practice on one color at a time. Take note of how that color makes you feel when you see it. This will help connect your ability to feel energy with your ability to see a person's aura. Additionally, practice seeing the sheets of paper out of your peripheral vision. This will develop your ability to see color outside your focused line of sight. You can take one day or even one week per color, depending on how quickly you feel your senses are developing.

The final phase for developing the ability to see and read auras is to practice on a friend. Have your friend sit across from you in a low-lit room. Avoid windows, as daylight can create color fluctuations in the room. Also, have them wear neutral colors, even black, as this will make the colors of their aura pop out more, making it easier for you to see. For best results, you can have them stand in front of a neutral-colored wall, about fifteen inches from you. Once in place, begin to focus on the wall next to them, about a couple inches from their body. As you focus, take note of your feelings. Do you feel happy, sad, nervous, or something else? When you determine the feel of their energy, you know what color to look for. Allow your focus to soften; thus, bringing your attention to your periphery vision. At this point, you must remain open-minded. If you think you see a color, any color at all, accept it. Don't question it, don't dismiss it, and don't look for something different. By accepting what you see, you open your mind and senses to the experience, thereby increasing your ability to see their aura. The more you practice this technique, the easier seeing auras will become. Eventually, you will see them anywhere at any time, regardless of environmental conditions.

Chapter 9: Healing

If you ask the average person on the street what superpower they would most like to have, you will hear a wide range of answers. Many would choose to fly, be super strong, or be able to access unlimited knowledge. A select few, in contrast, would choose to be able to heal people, mostly just by touching them. While this sounds about as unlikely a power to achieve as the ability to fly or punch through stone walls, the fact is that healing is another psychic ability, one that thousands of people possess all around the world. Unfortunately, few of these people are even aware of their gift, and fewer still know how to harness it, strengthen it, and put it to good use. This chapter will discuss several forms of psychic healing, showing how it is very much a part of holistic medicine in the modern world. Additionally, it will reveal how to determine whether or not you are a born healer, one gifted with the skill sets needed to be able to heal a person with a single touch. Finally, it will discuss how to strengthen your inherent skills, thus enabling you to have the healing effect on the world that you so desperately crave.

What is Psychic Healing?

The first thing to explore is the true nature of psychic healing. While most people turn to physical sources, such as doctors and over the counter medicines, when they get sick, some prefer a more spiritual approach, one that taps into the healing power of energy. Physical treatments heal a person from the outside; in contrast, psychic healing brings health and wellbeing from within, healing the individual at the very root of the problem, not merely treating the symptoms. This system is based on one simple truth: namely, that a person's physical, mental, and emotional health and wellbeing are all affected by the condition of their energy. When a person's energies are out of balance or blocked, physical and emotional illness will result. Thus, psychic healing is the practice of restoring proper balance and flow to a person's energies, thereby healing all sickness and suffering by fixing the actual cause on the spirit level.

There are numerous forms of psychic healing, each with their own unique methods and techniques for achieving the ultimate goal of total health and wellbeing. While some focus on a general approach, such as channeling the Universal life force into a person to recharge their energies, others have a more fine-tuned approach, focusing on the role of chakras and their performance when it comes to producing and maintaining energy. Subsequently, numerous tools and practices can be employed, each forming a specific tradition within the overall scope of psychic healing. This creates the same situation as that found in mediumship—namely, that not all psychic healers can practice all forms of psychic healing. Therefore, it is not only vital to discover whether or not you have the skill sets required for psychic healing in general, but it is also necessary to discover exactly what type of psychic healing is right for you.

Signs that you are a Psychic Healer

As with all psychic abilities, everyone has the potential to achieve some level of skill in this practice. However, those lacking inherent skills will struggle to produce even the most menial of results. Therefore, this is not a psychic ability recommended for just anyone. It is one that should only be pursued by an individual who demonstrates the qualities necessary for attracting and channeling healing energies in a significant and meaningful way. Fortunately, the signs for these qualities are easy to spot, making it easy to determine if psychic healing is your inherent gift. The following is a list of signs that will determine whether or not you have the traits of a natural-born healer:

1. You tend to feel deep empathy for others.
2. People close to you tend to remain in good overall health.
3. People tend to confide in you concerning their problems and pains.
4. Children and animals feel safe around you, even when they are skittish around other people.
5. You prefer to spend time alone in peaceful settings.
6. You are highly sensitive to the feelings and suffering of others.
7. Your dreams convey messages regarding sickness or healing in your body.
8. More than anything, you desire to help and heal others in any way possible.
9. You prefer spending time in nature, away from the hustle and bustle of humanity.
10. You prefer to listen to others rather than speak.
11. You have a deep interest in spirituality and have experienced events of awakening from time to time.
12. Medications and drugs don't often affect you the same way they affect others.
13. You have healers in your family, such as parents or grandparents.

If you identify with half or more of these statements, then the chances are that you are a natural-born healer. The next step is to identify the different types of healing so that you know which path to follow in your quest to develop your inherent skills.

The Role of Energy in Psychic Healing

As already mentioned, energy plays a huge role, both in terms of illness as well as psychic healing. Only when you understand the significance of energy can you begin to hone your abilities, thereby developing the healing touch you were meant to have. It should be mentioned again that sickness and distress are caused by an imbalance of energy in the individual. Sometimes this imbalance can be the result of physical trauma; however, more often than not, it is the result of emotional or spiritual trauma. Stress, for example, can significantly hinder the efficiency of chakras, thus reducing the flow of energy within a person's body. This will lead to such things as sore muscles, low levels of physical energy, and the increased likelihood of becoming ill. Rather than addressing those symptoms with traditional medicines and treatments, psychic healers know that the best way is to restore the balance and flow of energy within the patient, thereby restoring their natural ability to eliminate sickness and disease.

The main way that the energy of the patient is restored is by channeling healing energies into their body. This can come in two forms. First, the healer can use his or her own energy, often referred to as "ki" or "prana", to help boost the energy levels of the patient, much like jump-starting a car with a dead battery. By sending their energy into the patient, a healer can restore the patient's energy to a level where they will be able to return to a normal state of health and wellbeing. The downside of this is that the healer will become depleted if they have patients needing large amounts of energy in order to recover or in the case where they treat multiple patients within a given period. Subsequently, a healer must take the time to recharge their own energies in between sessions to ensure their own health and wellbeing.

The second form of energy healing is that of channeling, where the healer draws not from their personal energy, but rather from the healing energy of the Universe itself. In this case, the healer acts much like a medium, but instead of channeling a message from a spirit, they channel energy from the Universe. In a way, they act as an extension cord, connecting the patient with the source of energy that will restore their health and wellbeing. The positive side to this form is that it doesn't draw on the energy of the healer, meaning it won't deplete the healer's energy levels in the process. Furthermore, some techniques make it possible for the patient to channel the energy themselves, thereby enabling them to act as their own healer.

Common Forms of Psychic Healing

Just as there are many different specialties within the medical field, each focusing on a specific form of health and recovery, so too, there are several types of psychic healing. Each of the types can be classified into three categories. The first is what is known as Spiritual Healing. This is when a healer invokes the energies of the Universe to enter the body of the patient, thereby restoring the individual's energy levels, and thus their health and wellbeing. An example of Spiritual Healing is Reiki, an Ancient Japanese healing technique in which the healer channels ki energy to the patient, using their hands as the outlet for that energy. Some practitioners place their hands directly on the patient, while others keep them several inches over the patient's body. The name Reiki comes from the Japanese meaning Universal Power (Rei) and Energy (ki), signifying the source of the healing energy the practitioner channels to the patient.

Another type of Spiritual Healing is the use of crystals for restoring the energy levels in a patient. This practice focuses on restoring energy to the chakras, using the unique crystal associated with the specific chakra. For example, if a person has a throat issue, or is having trouble speaking, then their throat chakra needs to have its energies restored. Crystals such as aquamarine or sodalite will be placed on the patient to attract the necessary frequency of energy. The blue color of the crystals reflects the blue color of the chakra, and thus the frequency of the energy associated with it. The advantage of this practice is that the healer doesn't need to act as a channel for the energy to travel through, so there is no wear and tear on them as such. Additionally, the patient can actually perform the healing act themselves if they know what crystals to use for the chakra needing to be restored.

The second category of psychic healing is Pranic Healing. Originating in India, this form of healing incorporates the life force of the healer, otherwise known as the ki or the Prana. Unlike Spiritual Healing, which uses the life force of the Universe, this is where the healer will use their energy, much like the example mentioned above regarding jump-starting a car. Quantum Healing is an example of Pranic Healing. This is where the healer uses specific techniques to increase their own Prana, thereby enabling them to provide the energy necessary to restore the patient to health. Breathing techniques, body awareness techniques, and a special awareness of the different frequencies of energy come into play, allowing the healer to know which energies need restoring and how to increase those energies within themselves. They also know what symptoms to look for when determining deficient energies, much like a doctor would use physical symptoms to diagnose a disease.

The third category of psychic healing is Mental Healing. This is where the healer uses their mind to both diagnose and treat the patient. In a way, this is almost a form of telepathic healing, whereby the healer taps into the subconscious of the patient in order to determine the nature of the illness and then uses their mind to envision the healing process, sending that image into the subconscious of the patient like a program of sorts. When done correctly, the healer can virtually instruct the patient to get better just by using their telepathic abilities. Needless to say, this is the rarest of the three categories, requiring the highest levels of intuition, telepathy, and clairvoyance that a person can achieve.

Two other methods of healing focus more on the correction of energy flow rather than the introduction of healing energy. These are the Chinese forms of healing known as acupuncture and acupressure. Acupuncture is the practice of using special needles to draw out negative energy that blocks the flow of healthy energy throughout the body. It focuses on the fourteen meridians of energy flow, discovering where blockages are located and releasing those blockages through the needles. While this practice looks painful, the patient barely feels the needles at all. Instead, they feel the release of tension, which restores proper energy flow to their body once again.

Acupressure acts in much the same way, except that it utilizes pressure instead of needles. The healer will use his or her fingers to apply pressure to the affected parts of the body, thus releasing tension and restoring proper energy flow to the patient. Needless to say, in both cases, the healer has to have the intuition needed to know where the blockages are, as well as how to release them. Still, where these treatments differ is that the healer does not send energy into the patient; rather, they release the patient's energy, thereby restoring overall health and wellbeing to the individual.

How to Develop your Psychic Healing Skills

When it comes to developing your healing skills, the best method is practice, practice, and more practice. Of course, the first step is determining which type of psychic healing is best for you. To do this, you want to find practitioners from each discipline and talk to them about your desire to become a healer. These people will know what it takes to perform their specific variety of psychic healing, so they will be able to tell whether you are a good fit or not. Furthermore, they will take you under their wing and teach you the ropes, further testing your natural abilities. If you struggle to make progress in one particular discipline, it might mean you need to try another. Eventually, you will find your niche, feeling your skills rise within you as you begin to learn and develop the techniques of the healing form that is right for you.

Chapter 10: Contacting and Communicating with your Spirit Guides

The final and perhaps most exciting psychic ability to explore is communicating with spirit guides. While all psychic abilities are amazing and wonderful, communicating with spirit guides takes the psychic experience to the next level, literally. Spirit guides have been a part of human culture since prehistoric times, with shamanic practices still relying on the knowledge and insights of spirits in many African and South American cultures to this very day. Even the major religions of the world, including Judaism, Islam, and Christianity, contain rich and varied traditions when it comes to spirit guides and the forms they can take. The bottom line is that just about every spiritual tradition believes that spirits exist to help and guide people through every aspect of their Earthly existence.

Unfortunately, many people fail to recognize the messages their guides are trying to send them, resulting in them blindly making their way through life, making needless mistakes and missing countless opportunities. For those who discover and listen to those messages, the results are vastly different. Those are the people who can avoid most pitfalls and know when to embark on new and exciting adventures. This chapter will discuss the different types of spirit guides that exist, helping you to recognize those sent to help you along your path. Furthermore, it will reveal ways to discover and contact your personal guides, creating a rich and meaningful relationship with them—one that will change your life in ways most people can't even imagine.

What are Spirit Guides?

The first thing to address is the true nature of spirit guides. Perhaps the best way to explain what they are is to consider one of the most common images of them in use today, specifically that of an angel. The word "angel" comes from the Ancient Greek word "angelos", which translates as a messenger. This dismisses the idea that angels are fat babies rolling around in clouds, or harp loving musicians passing the time singing in long white robes while humanity struggles far below. As messengers, angels are spirits that not only observe humanity closely, but also try to give advice, warnings, and encouragement to those who would listen. You can take this one step further by factoring in the common belief in guardian angels, suggesting that not only are angels sent to advise, but they are also tasked with protecting a certain individual from harm whenever possible.

Fortunately, you don't have to subscribe to a particular religion in order to discover and communicate with your spirit guide. Such guides exist no matter what your belief system is. Even atheists have spirit guides assigned to them, meaning that you don't have to earn their help; you simply have to accept it. Furthermore, spirit guides can take many different shapes and forms, each possessing unique qualities and benefits that are usually tailored for the individual they serve. The following are some of the most common forms of spirit guides, along with the basic nature of their role in your life:

> • **Angels:** As mentioned, angels are the messengers of the spirit realm. Often seen in terms of the counterpart to demons, they can advise you to choose the right path when temptation entices you to choose the wrong path—one that will prove dangerous and ultimately disastrous. Archangels

are the highest form of angels, considered the most proficient and powerful. Some archangels are fairly well known through stories and traditions, including Michael, Gabriel, and Rafael. If you are lucky enough to be in contact with an archangel, you can be assured that your future is very promising indeed!

• **Ancestors:** Another common tradition held throughout the world and human history is the idea that deceased relatives can play a role in guiding and protecting their loved ones in this life. This is particularly true in the case of departed parents or grandparents, people who had a very close and vested interest in you while they were still alive. The belief here is that their love keeps them close to you for a while, enabling them to send encouragement and love in times of distress or general loneliness.

• **Spirit Animals:** Almost everyone has heard the term "totem animal" used in one context or another. Unfortunately, most people have only experienced totem animals in terms of online quizzes that are for entertainment purposes only. The truth is that spirit animals serve a much greater purpose than merely fodder for party conversations. They can give you the elemental strength and courage you need to face even the most daunting of challenges, bringing out your best "nature" when you need it the most.

• **Deities:** Ancient societies worshipped many gods and goddesses, something not commonly done in modern times. One of the reasons for this is that it allowed the ancients to contemplate the various aspects of humanity. Zeus, for example, could serve to embody leadership, fatherly love, and the wisdom of an older person. Aphrodite, in contrast, represented physical beauty and carnal pleasure. Thus, each deity could appear to the individual in order to reinforce certain elements of that person's character. If you start seeing visions of gods or goddesses, rather than being a construct of your imagination, it could be a real message—one providing you with the answers you need.

- **Religious Figures:** Many people around the world have claimed to have seen visions or heard messages from Jesus, Mary, the Buddha, and other such religious figures. While some of these claims may be hoaxes, many are probably the real deal, suggesting that the spirits of these once corporeal souls are still trying to influence people, leading them along the right path when times are tough and hard choices need to be made.

- **Sacred Figures:** Almost all spiritual traditions have sacred figures of one form or another. Priests, shamans, popes, elders, and wisdom women help lead the practitioners of their tradition while on Earth. What many don't realize is that they continue to serve in this capacity even when departed. It is as though their soul continues to fulfill their calling despite their body being long gone. Having a sacred figure as a spirit guide is not only a gift beyond measure; it is a chance for you to access all of the knowledge that guides spend a lifetime discovering.

How to Detect your Spirit Guides

Now that you have an idea as to the different types of spirit guides and the forms they take, the next step is to detect the spirit guide or guides that are trying to help you live the best life possible. This is where your psychic abilities will prove themselves more useful than ever. The bottom line is that spirit guides are just that— spirits. Therefore, you can't expect to see, hear, or experience them with your physical senses—at least not at first. Instead, you have to tap into your psychic senses, your clairs, and use them to detect your spirit guides with your inner eye, inner ear, or whatever inner sense is strongest for you.

Not surprisingly, dreams are an ideal way to detect your spirit guides. This is because dreams are nothing but internal, meaning your inner senses are at their highest level since your physical senses are quite literally asleep. There are two ways in which your dreams can reveal the identity of your spirit guides. First, try to recall your dreams from the past, especially when you were struggling with difficult issues in the waking world. Did you dream of a religious figure coming to offer you encouragement or support? Perhaps a dream character shows up regularly, especially when you are struggling the most. Or have specific animals been in your dreams, awakening your primal energies for the challenges at hand? If you have had any such dreams, recognize them as nothing less than an encounter with your spirit guide. Needless to say, write these dreams down immediately, much the way you would the name and phone number of someone you just met.

The second way dreams can help detect your spirit guide is through the process of dream incubation. This is where you spend time just before going to sleep telling yourself to have dreams of a specific sort. For example, if you wanted to dream about being rich and famous, you would meditate on the specifics before falling asleep, creating the dream environment for you to realize your fantasies. This same process can be used to discover the identity of your spirit guides. In this case, take the time before falling asleep to meditate on a particular place, like a café or a park bench. Imagine your spirit guide meeting you there. They may already be there, or they may come and find you. In any event, when you find yourself on that park bench, don't dismiss the first person who sits next to you as they are probably your spirit guide.

Synchronicity is another common way in which spirit guides can send messages. Therefore, if you want to know who your spirit guide is, ask for a pattern to emerge in your waking life. For example, if you see numerous images of angels throughout your day, including pictures, statues, and other forms, then take that as the answer. If you see images of a particular deity or the name of a deity, then don't dismiss that as coincidence. Animals can also present themselves—although don't imagine that your totem animal is a squirrel if you spend the day in a park where squirrels are a dime a dozen. What you are looking for are signs that are out of the ordinary. If you see images of lions all day long, then that might be the answer you seek. But don't go to the zoo looking for inspiration.

If you are faced with information overload and don't know whether you are seeing a pattern or mere coincidence, there are two things you can do to solve the confusion. First, take a couple of days off and try again later when your mind is open and your heart ready. When you see the same signs or images repeat, then you have your answer. The second thing is to turn to your gut feeling. Although the signs are physical, the message is still psychic in nature; therefore, you should feel it as well as see it. If the pattern resonates within your soul, then you know you have your answer. However, if you don't feel a connection or a good feeling about what you are observing, then it is probably just a fluke, and you can ignore it, looking elsewhere for your sign to appear.

How to Communicate with your Spirit Guides

When it comes to communicating with your spirit guides, the best approach is to treat it as though you are developing a relationship with them. When you strip away the details, such as the nature of your spirit guides or the role they play in your life, what you are left with is the dynamic of creating a strong, caring and even loving relationship. Therefore, treat the process of creating a relationship with your spirit guides the same way that you would if you were creating a relationship with a significant other. The first step is to talk to them regularly. Even if you don't hear them respond at first, talk to them as much as you can. Don't just turn to them for help in your time of need. Chat with them daily. Tell them how happy you are that they are there. Ask them how their day is. Even though this may seem ridiculous, at first, the more you talk to your guides, the stronger your connection will become. This means that you will hear them better when you need to call on them for help, so it is not just about having fun; it's also about developing certain vital skill sets.

The next step is to take the time to listen. You might choose to meditate to tune in to your spirit guides, or you might simply pause after you ask a question or make a statement in order to hear the message they have in response. This is a good opportunity to discover how your spirit guides choose to communicate with you. If you are skilled with clairaudience, then the chances are that they will choose to speak to you, so you must take the time to sit in a quiet place and listen for their voice. Alternatively, they may be the sort of spirits that use signs to get their message across. If, for example, you want to know the name of your guardian angel, then after you ask the question, take the time to listen. If you hear a name pop into your head, go with it, even if it's disappointing, at first. Not everyone can have Archangel Michael as their guide. Yours might, in fact, be Bob or Sue. Don't be snobbish and dismiss the name, waiting for something better.

However, if you don't hear a name, start looking for one. Look for names on billboards, TV ads, restaurant signs, and the like. Don't go through the phonebook looking for the name that sounds right; let the name come to you. That is the point of listening, after all. Have faith that your spirit guide is capable enough to get a message across to you if you put in the effort to try and hear what they have to say. Using synchronicity is a good way to confirm the name you heard in your head in the event you had an audio response. For example, if you heard the name Rose, then take the time to look for confirmation throughout the day. Ask for signs to confirm the message. You never know, you might receive a bouquet of roses out of the blue, telling you that you heard the name of your spirit guide loud and clear. This may seem farfetched, and even silly to the newcomer, but anyone with experience in communicating with spirit guides will tell you that they often love to use humor, making you smile while conveying the message you need to hear. In fact, you can think of it as them showing off their skills, or rewarding you for your efforts by treating you to something meaningful and fun.

This method of asking and listening is the same method you will use whether you ask your spirit guides for their name or for guidance on making an important decision at hand. However, when it comes to issues that have a "yes or no" quality to them, you can fall back on gut feeling. You don't need to spend the day listening for a voice to say yes or no, nor do you need to look for the first answer that presents itself in plain sight. Instead, listen to your heart. This is where your psychic communication takes place anyway. Therefore, if someone offers you a job, for example, clear your mind, ask your guides whether this is the right move, and then feel the answer. If you feel uplifted, even euphoric, then that is them telling you to go for it. Alternatively, if you feel anxious or even a sense of dread, then graciously decline the offer, knowing that your guides have spared you future hardship and pain.

Ways to Develop your Ability to Communicate with your Spirit Guides

The final thing you will want to do is to strengthen your ability to communicate with your spirit guides. Again, one of the best ways to achieve this goal is to practice every day, just like you would when trying to improve any other psychic ability or any ability at all for that matter. The more you practice, the better you will get; it's really that simple. Therefore, start by talking and listening to your guides, asking simple and basic questions, at first, such as what form they take and what they wish to be called. The more time and effort you spend asking the easy questions, the better prepared you will be when it comes to tackling the more important issues.

The next thing you need to do is keep a journal. This is a critical practice in developing any psychic skill set. In this case, you will want to record all of the messages you receive. Write down the message itself, such as a name or an answer to a question. Then write down the form the message took. Did you hear it, see it or dream it? No matter how it came to you, write it down. Finally, write down whether the message proved to be true or not. In the beginning, you will find that many of the messages you hear are products of your thoughts and imagination. It takes time to sort out the voices of your guides from the other thoughts and ideas in your head. That is why you want to keep a journal. Eventually, a pattern will develop, one that shows the method by which you have had the most success. For example, if your dreams prove spot on every time, then focus on your dreams as your primary source of communication. Research dream dynamics and do everything you can to be the best when it comes to creating, experiencing, and recalling your dreams. If the answers you hear are the ones that prove more accurate, then take the time and effort to develop clairaudience. In the end, use your journal as a learning tool, one that will show you what works best and what doesn't. You can also use your journal to help keep track of ways to develop your skills once you have discovered your spirit guides' chosen form of communication.

Finally, ask for help. As with any relationship, both parties need to be on the same page. If you want to know how your spirit guides choose to communicate, ask them. This should be one of the first questions you ask—if not the absolute first. After all, only when you know how to find the answers will it make sense to ask any other questions. Once you know the form of communication your guides prefer, you can ask them what you need to do in order to improve your ability to communicate with them. You might find an advertisement on TV that provides inspiration, or a billboard might have a statement that hits home. In the end, your spirit guides are there to help you succeed, so they won't make it difficult. All you need to do is be patient with yourself, allowing yourself time to learn while not getting frustrated at the mistakes you make. Always keep an open mind and never give up. Developing a relationship with spirits won't always be easy, even if it is your personal psychic gift. However, the rewards that such a relationship can provide will be beyond measure, making the time and effort more worthwhile than you can possibly imagine. Once you develop a rich and meaningful relationship with your spirit guides, you will never again have to face another day alone. And that in and of itself can be enough to change your life completely, enabling you to live the happy, loving, and fulfilling life you both desire and deserve.

Conclusion

Now that you have read this book, you have all the tools you need to identify and develop your personal psychic abilities. Whether you are a natural-born healer, a clairvoyant, or a medium able to channel messages from departed souls, you can begin to hone your skills so that you can use your abilities to live a life of untold wonder and purpose. Furthermore, by following the instructions on meditation and general practices for improving mental and physical wellbeing, you will improve your life on every level. This will help reduce your stress, improve your energy levels, and provide you with the peace of mind you truly deserve. Finally, once you develop the ability to clear your mind of the clutter of day-to-day life, you will be able to tap into the spirit realm in ways you never imagined possible. Whether it's seeing events before they unfold, hearing the thoughts of a loved one miles away, or even speaking to spirit guides, you will discover abilities and talents that transcend physical reality, taking your life experience to a whole new dimension. The very best of luck to you as you embark on your journey of exploring and developing your psychic abilities.

Your Free Gift (only available for a limited time)

Thanks for getting this book! If you want to learn more about various spirituality topics, then join Mari Silva's community and get a free guided meditation MP3 for awakening your third eye. This guided meditation mp3 is designed to open and strengthen ones third eye so you can experience a higher state of consciousness. Simply visit the link below the image to get started.

https://spiritualityspot.com/meditation

Sources

https://psychicelements.com/blog/psychic-abilities/

https://www.keen.com/articles/psychic/psychic-intuitive-medium-whats-the-difference

https://www.aetherius.org.nz/develop-intuition-psychic-abilities/

https://www.amazon.com/Psychic-Development-Beginners-Naturally-Intuition-ebook/dp/B00YCBT838/ref=sr_1_5?keywords=psychic+development+for+beginners&qid=1572852362&sr=8-5

https://www.psychicgurus.org/5-fun-activities-for-psychic-development/

https://intuitivesoulsblog.com/develop-your-psychic-abilities/

https://www.psychicgurus.org/psychic-meditation/

https://www.psychicperformer.com/4-spiritual-practices-that-can-improve-your-psychic-connection/

https://www.amazon.com/Discover-Your-Psychic-Type-Developing/dp/0738712787/ref=sr_1_6?crid=136JF0LCTW3AN&keywords=developing+psychic+abilities&qid=1572989803&s=books&sprefix=developing+psychic+%2Caps%2C435&sr=1-6

https://www.annasayce.com/which-is-your-strongest-intuitive-gift/

https://www.psychologytoday.com/us/blog/debunking-myths-the-mind/201804/the-biology-telepathy

https://www.psychicgurus.org/how-to-read-minds-telepathically/

https://www.oprah.com/spirit/what-is-a-medium-rebecca-rosen

https://www.amandalinettemeder.com/blog/2014/12/23/7-steps-to-improve-your-mediumship-abilities

https://www.psychicgurus.org/psychometry/

https://www.gaia.com/article/how-to-see-auras

https://www.psychicgurus.org/psychic-healing/

https://www.psychokinesispowers.com/psychic-healing-techniques

https://www.ncbi.nlm.nih.gov/pmc/articles/PMC4107996/

https://intuitivesoulsblog.com/psychic-development-tip-2-meet-spirit-guides/

https://www.erinpavlina.com/blog/2006/11/connecting-with-spirit-guides/

https://www.huffpost.com/entry/encounters-with-psychics_n_56c4c530e4b0b40245c8b5b1

https://liveanddare.com/types-of-meditation/

https://www.annasayce.com/the-forgotten-clairs-clairgustance-and-clairsalience/

https://www.huffpost.com/entry/the-habits-of-highly-intu_n_4958778

https://www.heysigmund.com/9-ways-to-tap-into-your-intuition-and-why-youll-want-to/

https://www.bustle.com/p/11-ways-to-know-if-your-intuition-is-trying-to-tell-you-something-how-to-listen-38787

https://www.poweredbyintuition.com/2013/04/28/13-examples-of-intuition-in-everyday-life from-top-creatives/

http://beyondiam.com/examples-of-intuition/

https://consciouslifenews.com/7-easy-ways-develop-telepathic-abilities/11103458/#

https://www.headspace.com/meditation/techniques

https://forums.forteana.org/index.php?threads/smoke-billets-pictures-from-the-other-side.52237/

https://www.amandalinettemeder.com/blog/the-4-main-types-of-mediumship

https://www.psychologytoday.com/us/blog/neuronarrative/201212/study-finds-the-unexpected-in-the-brains-spirit-mediums-0

https://www.color-meanings.com/spiritual-colors-the-difference-between-auras-and-chakras/

https://aura.net/chakras-auras-work-together/

https://www.psychics4today.com/how-to-see-auras/

https://www.gaia.com/article/what-is-a-spirit-guide

https://www.speakingtree.in/allslides/the-scientific-evidence-of-human-aura

https://gostica.com/aura-science/layers-of-the-aura/#:~:targetText=Energy%20body%20(or%20aura)%20has,and%20the%20immediate%20external%20environment.&targetText=Each%20layer%20or%20level%20is%20an%20energy%20field%20varying%20in%20vibration.

Printed in Great Britain
by Amazon